Simple Sermons for Sunday Evening

Simple Sermons for Sunday Evening

W. Herschel Ford

BAKER BOOK HOUSE
Grand Rapids, Michigan 49516

Copyright 1967 by Zondervan Publishing House
Grand Rapids, Michigan

Reprinted 1988 by Baker Book House
Grand Rapids, Michigan
with the permission of the copyright holder

Library of Congress Catalog Card Number: 67-22685
ISBN: 0-8010-3545-7

Second printing, July 1989

Printed in the United States of America

DEDICATION

This book is dedicated with great affection to Dr. and Mrs. A. G. Williams, of Pasadena, Texas, dear and precious friends of mine, faithful and devoted followers of the Lord Jesus Christ.

Foreword

This is my twenty-fourth volume of Simple Sermons. Why do I continue writing these books? Let me give you just one instance in answer to that question.

A Hindu priest in Rhodesia came to know Christ through the ministry of one of our missionaries. God called him to preach the Gospel. He wrote me that, since he had no homiletical or theological training, he took one of my sermons and memorized it and then preached it to his people. He said he had witnessed the salvation of souls and the changing of lives through this second-hand ministry.

I pray that many other servants of God will use my messages in the same way for God's glory and the salvation of souls.

W. HERSCHEL FORD

Contents

1. The Name Above Every Name 13
2. Christians Are Sitting Pretty 22
3. Put a Ring on His Finger 31
4. Jesus Calls Us 40
5. Lost Horizons 50
6. The Best Things in Life 60
7. Heaven's Theme Song 69
8. Though Your Sins Be as Scarlet 77
9. The Question We Never Ask 86
10. The Doctrine of the New Birth 97
11. Jesus Highest Over All 109
12. What Jesus Means to Me 118

Simple Sermons for Sunday Evening

1

The Name Above Every Name
Philippians 2:5-11

Shakespeare tells us that there is nothing in a name. He says that if a rose were called by any other name it would smell just as sweet. In a sense, however, he is wrong. If I were to give you a check I had signed, a check for a million dollars, it would be worthless. But a similar check, bearing the name of a Rockefeller would be of great value to you.

Names do mean something. When you hear the name of Moses you think of the great leader and law-giver. The name of David brings to mind the shepherd boy who became a king, the poet who wrote the twenty-third Psalm. The name of Solomon makes us think of wisdom and wealth. Wesley's name causes us to think of the founder of Methodism. Henry Ford's name reminds us of the automobile industry, while the name of Spurgeon reminds us of the great London preacher of another day.

Yes, names do mean something. We ought to place a high value upon our names and live in such a way as never to bring reproach upon that name. The Bible tells us that "a good name is rather to be chosen than great riches" (Proverbs 22:1). Let us so live, then, that when people hear our names they will be reminded of goodness and usefulness and Christ Himself.

But today I present to you the greatest name that ever graced heaven, the noblest name ever spoken upon this earth. This name has been spoken by every tongue, every tribe, every race. It has been lisped by baby lips and praised in the great affairs of men. It has been whispered in the hour of death. It is the blessed, wonderful name of Jesus.

> "Jesus," O how sweet the name!
> "Jesus," every day the same;
> "Jesus," let all saints proclaim
> Its worthy praise forever.

I. His Name Is a Saving Name

Before Jesus' birth the angel said to Joseph, "Thou shalt call his name Jesus: for he shall save his people from their sins" (Matthew 1:21). Jesus was a Teacher, a Preacher, a Healer, an Example, but primarily He was and is a Saviour.

1. *He said He would save us.* He said, "Look unto me, and be ye saved, all the ends of the earth" (Isaiah 45:22). When we think of the ends of the earth, we think of those places farthest removed from us. This text surely then refers to those far removed from God. It means that the lowest, vilest sinner in all the world is invited to come unto Jesus and be saved.

The Bible says, "Though your sins be as scarlet, they shall be as white as snow" (Isaiah 1:18). The Bible also says, "The Son of man is come to seek and to save that which was lost" (Luke 19:10). Paul said, "This is a faithful saying, and worthy of all acceptation, that Christ Jesus came into the world to save sinners" (I Timothy 1:15). Jesus said, "Him that cometh to me I will in no wise cast out" (John 6:37).

Throughout the Bible the Lord is promising to save all who come unto Him through Christ. Men may break their promises, but Jesus, never. Every man in every age who has come to Christ has been gloriously saved.

2. *He has saved many of us.* We have felt the power of the Holy Spirit in conviction. He has pointed us to the

Lamb of God, who alone can save. We have repented of our sins and put our trust in Him, and now we have the assurance in our hearts that we are the children of God. Satan often causes us to doubt our salvation. When he does we need to take him back to our conversion experience and say to him, "What about that?" We know that Christ has saved us and that Satan can never get us. "The blood of Jesus Christ his Son cleanseth us from all sin" (I John 1:7).

General O. O. Howard was gloriously saved one night in a revival service. The next morning, as he rejoiced in his new-found salvation, another officer said to him, "General, I can show you a dozen inconsistencies in the Bible." The general replied, "You may show me those things, but you cannot prove to me that I did not give my heart to Christ and you cannot prove to me that He didn't save me. I know I am His and He is mine."

3. *He has saved others.* In the long ago an English bartender was dealing out damnation in his saloon. But one day Christ came into that man's heart and life. God called him to preach and he went up and down all of England, preaching the Gospel. He came to America and led thousands of souls to the Saviour. It is said that 70,000 persons were converted under his ministry. His name was George Whitefield.

How can you account for such men? How can you account for Dwight L. Moody, for Billy Sunday, for Billy Graham, for Robert G. Lee and thousands of others? The answer is altogether in Jesus, the mighty Saviour. Look at your own life. Once you were on the downward path of sin. You despised the things of Christ and His Church. But now all of this is changed. You love that which you once hated, you hate that which you once loved. What created the change? It was the saving name of Jesus. Yes, "Jesus is the sweetest name I know."

II. His Name Is a Precious Name

Peter said, "Unto you therefore which believe he is precious" (I Peter 2:7). He is not precious to unbelievers, He is a reproach to them. But He is most precious to His own. The name of wife or mother or sweetheart or child is precious, but the name of Jesus is the most precious name of all.

1. *He is precious because of what He has done.* He picked us up out of the muck and mire of sin and made us to become sons of God. Lincoln was born in a log cabin, but destiny lifted him into the highest office in the land. From a poor preacher's manse Woodrow Wilson was lifted up to the same office and Herbert Hoover came up from a blacksmith's cottage. But Jesus Christ has done more than that for us. He has had mercy upon us in our low estate and has lifted us up to a position higher than the angels.

Someone once asked Sir James Simpson, the great scientist, "What is the greatest discovery you ever made?" And the humble Christian answered, "My greatest discovery came when I learned that I was a sinner and that Jesus Christ had become my Saviour."

2. *He is precious because of what He is doing now.* He is keeping us in the hollow of His hands. He saved us and now He is keeping us. One day as Jesus passed through Jericho He saw a little man by the name of Zaccheus up in a sycamore tree. He called Zaccheus down and gave him eternal life. An old legend tells us that in later life Zaccheus would go out each morning to that tree. He would water its roots and pull up the weeds around it. Then, putting his arms around the tree, he would say, "This is the tree which brought me to the One whom my soul loveth."

It would help us if we would often go back down memory lane and kneel at the foot of the cross and live over again our experience, knowing that He who saved us is still keeping us. We are His sheep and He will never let us perish. We are His children to whom He has given eternal life.

What else is He doing now? He is answering our prayers. Every child of God can say, "I know that He has often answered my prayers." Yonder in the middle of the ocean a ship is sinking. The wireless operator sends out his appeal for help, but no other ship is near enough to hear and to help. It is not so with Jesus. He is always near to hear and help.

What else is He doing? He is interceding for us. "He ever liveth to make intercession for them" (Hebrews 7:25). Here is a man who is to go on trial before the court on a certain date. He knows he is guilty and that he will be assessed a large fine, and he has no money. But when he reaches the courtroom he learns that his fine has been paid by a friend, so he goes out rejoicing.

Someone has interceded for him and he is grateful. Well, Jesus does just that for us. We are guilty of many things, but through His intercession the penalty is removed and we are set free.

3. *He is precious because of what He will do.* He said, "I go to prepare a place for you, And if I go and prepare a place for you, I will come again, and receive you unto myself, that where I am, there ye may be also." The Bible tells us that we have not seen or heard or even imagined all the good things that God has in store for us. We don't know all about heaven, but we know that it will be a place of complete satisfaction, a place of everlasting bliss.

A young man says to his bride-to-be, "I am building a house for you. I will build it exactly to your tastes and needs. When it is finished I will show it to you." Then the glad day comes when the house is finished. He carries her out to see it. She hurries through every room in a fever of excitement, then she says, "Darling, it is beautiful, it is wonderful, it is far more than I expected." And when we get to heaven we'll feel the same way. We will say, "O Jesus, it is far more wonderful than I ever dreamed it could be. The half was never told me."

III. His Name Is a Comforting Name

Before Christ went back to heaven He said, "Let not your heart be troubled, just put all of your trust in Me." Oh, there are many times in our lives when our hearts are troubled and we need the comfort that only He can give.

1. *His name is a comfort in time of sorrow.* All of us have our black Fridays, all of us have walked down the valley of tears and sadness. Where do we find comfort in such an hour? Our worldly friends cannot give it to us. But when a friend of Jesus whispers His name into our ears, it is like soothing music to our hearts.

When the Bethany sisters lost their brother, Lazarus, they did the wise thing. They sent for Jesus. Somehow they knew that they would find comfort in Him. And, oh, He did far more for them than they hoped or dreamed.

Some years ago an acquaintance of mine died. He was a devoted Christian. Before he died he called his wife and children to his bedside. He had a prayer with them and urged them not to mourn for him when he went away. I attended the funeral and found there a scene of peace and holy submission. There was no rebellion, there was only a strong faith in God and His goodness. The peace of God was written upon the faces of his loved ones. Yes, God's people die well, and He gives comfort in the hour of sorrow.

2. *His Name is a comfort when we are dying.* If our Lord tarries the hour of dying is coming to every one of us. We're going to need Him then. We'll want to feel the touch of His hand upon ours as our feet reach the icy waters of the river of death.

A woman with a dark past was gloriously saved. When she came to the end of the way she said, "I lived a wicked life, but, oh, how sweet now to trust in Jesus and to know that I am going home with Him." Thank God, when that hour comes for us, we can feel the warm clasp of His hand and we can know that He will see us safely home.

IV. His Name Is a Conquering Name

1. *His name is conquering many in Judaism.* Often we hear of a Jew who has come to know that the Christ of the New Testament is the Messiah of the Old Testament. And what happy and active Christians they become, following in the footsteps of Saul who became Paul the mighty apostle.

2. *His name is conquering paganism and heathenism.* In the New Hebrides Islands there is a tablet on a Presbyterian church containing this inscription, "When Rev. John Geddie came here in 1846 there were no Christians on the island. When he left in 1872 there were no heathen." His name is conquering paganism and heathenism wherever that name is proclaimed.

3. *His name is conquering sinful hearts everywhere.* He does not conquer by the sword or the gun or the bomb. He conquers by love. He does not rail out at sinners; He loves them and wants to save them.

A long time ago a rebellious knight brandished his sword toward heaven and cried out in blasphemy against Christ. Suddenly the wind blew a piece of paper near his feet. He picked up the paper and read the words, "God Is Love." The man burst into tears and surrendered his all to Christ.

A preacher friend of mine was conducting a revival in a mountain community. A man who operated a "moonshine" liquor distillery came to the meeting and the Lord saved him. Then he asked the preacher, "What must I do with my still?" The preacher told him that he ought to sell it. "No," said the man, "if I did that I am afraid it would damn some other man. I'll just take my axe and hack it to pieces." Yes, the name of Jesus is a conquering name.

V. His Name Is and Will Be an Exalted Name

"God hath highly exalted him, and given him a name which is above every name" (Philippians 2:9).

Many names have been highly exalted in this old world. We think of Pharaoh and Alexander the Great and Caesar and Napoleon and Vanderbilt and Rockefeller and thousands of others. But there has never been a name like the name of Jesus. Other names have been exalted by men; His name is and will be exalted by God Himself.

Jesus Christ left heaven. He laid aside the cloak of royalty and came down to a world of sin and shame. Though He was rich, for our sakes He became poor. Here He was debased, He occupied the lowest position on earth. He had no wealth, no home, no family, no property. He died on a shameful cross. Then God said, "It is enough. He has suffered enough. He has gone low enough. I'll give Him a throne, I'll exalt His name and place it above every name."

The throne of heaven is vacant. Whom shall we place there? Abraham was the father of a mighty race, he was the friend of God, he was highly honored. But he has no right to that throne. Think of Moses and David and Solomon and John the Baptist and Paul. Think of Spurgeon and Moody, of Washington and Lincoln. Not one of these is worthy to sit upon that heavenly throne.

But Jesus came to earth and was slain upon a cross. He wore a peasant's garment, His hands were nailed to the tree, He wore a crown of thorns. But God changed all of that. When Jesus comes again He will sit upon a royal throne, His garments will be as white as snow, His face will be brighter than the sun, His hand will hold the scepter of universal dominion. Then the angels and the hosts of heaven will sing out:

> All hail the power of Jesus' name!
> Let angels prostrate fall;
> Bring forth the royal diadem,
> And crown Him Lord of all.

Then the crown will be placed upon His head, while the shout rings throughout the corridors of heaven, "God hath highly exalted him, and given him a name which is above every name."

Now what does this name mean to you? Have you called on Him as Saviour? Have you been washed in the blood? Have you surrendered to Him as Lord and Master? Does He reign in your heart? Is He precious to you? Is He all in all to you?

As a Christian woman lay dying someone whispered, "She's sinking." But she opened her eyes and said, "How can I sink? I am standing on the Rock of Ages." My friend, are you on the Solid Rock?

One Sunday morning Queen Victoria attended church and heard a sermon on the return of the Lord. As she thanked the preacher for the message, she said, "I wish that Christ would come in my lifetime." The preacher asked her why she had this desire, and she replied, "Because I would like to lay my crown at His blessed feet."

Oh, let us come and lay our all at His feet. Let us crown Him Lord of our lives.

2

Christians Are Sitting Pretty
I John 3:1-3

Dr. Donald Grey Barnhouse preached one Sunday morning on the joys of the Christian life. He told how our sins are washed away and of the wonderful blessings which are ours as the children of God. A boy who had been sitting in the balcony came down to speak to the preacher at the close of the service. He said, "Doc, that was a good sermon. Christians are sitting pretty, aren't they?" That was a strange way to put it, but surely the boy was right.

Doctors tell us that in the first few minutes of a baby's life at least forty physical changes take place. And as soon as a person is born again, some wonderful changes come to him, also. He becomes a child of God, which means a change of parentage. He becomes an heir of God, possessing a rich inheritance. He possesses eternal life, which means a change of destiny.

He is accepted in the beloved and is no longer a stranger to God. He is sealed by the Holy Spirit with a seal that cannot be broken. He becomes a temple of the Holy Spirit — God lives within him.

Now not one of these things is gained by anything we do. It is all the gift of God. The Christian is indeed sitting pretty.

I. CHRISTIANS ARE SITTING PRETTY BECAUSE OF WHAT GOD HAS DONE WITH THEIR SINS

1. *He has forgiven their sins.* All of our lives we have

been sinning. We are even born in sin and we stay in sin. There is a big heavenly record against us and we can't erase it. But what does God do? He takes the heavenly pen, dips it in the precious blood of the Lord Jesus Christ and writes one big word across the page, the word "forgiven."

That is wonderful. How does a man feel whose sins are not forgiven, who can't look up into God's face because of the shame of his sin? I don't know. I only know that it feels mighty good to know that your sins are forgiven and that you won't have to meet them again.

2. *He has forgotten our sins.* We often say, "I can forgive, but I cannot forget." But when God forgives, He also forgets. No longer does He remember our sins.

A little boy came into the house one morning and said to his mother, "I'm not going to play with Roland any more, I'm mad at him." But that afternoon he was out in the yard, playing with Roland and having a good time. Later his mother said to him, "I thought you were mad at Roland, and that you weren't going to play with him anymore." He answered, "Oh, Roland and me are good forgetters." They had completely forgotten the trouble of the morning.

But that is nothing compared to God. He is the greatest Forgetter. Sometimes, as we think of our sins, we dread the idea of coming before Him. But we are not to worry for He forgets our sins entirely.

3. *He has cleansed us from sin.* We are foul on the inside — sin has polluted us. But, thank God, "the blood of Jesus Christ his Son cleanses us from all sin" (I John 1:7). God forgives and forgets our sins, but if that was all He did, we would be left unclean. So He goes on to do a thorough job. He cleans us up.

4. *He has made atonement for our sins.* When Christ died, He took His own precious blood and offered it up to

the Father. He said, "I offer this blood as an atonement for the sins of the world." And God said, "It is enough, I accept it."

Although Christ died to atone for all the sins of mankind, there is no value whatsoever for a man in that atonement unless that man receives Christ as his personal Saviour. Our sins are atoned for only when we accept what Christ did for us on the cross.

> Jesus paid it all,
> All to Him I owe;
> Sin had left a crimson stain,
> He washed it white as snow.

5. *He has covered our sins.* All over the world there are buried treasures, and men spend time and money seeking these treasures. They seldom find them, for they are too well hidden. But when God covers our sins and buries them in His forgetfulness, no man on earth can ever dig them up.

6. *He has blotted out our sins.* The Bible tells us that He blots them out as a dark cloud. We often look up into the face of the sun, then suddenly a dark cloud moves over and the sun is completely blotted out. It is like this when God blots out our sins.

7. *He has cast our sins into the deepest sea.* This is just another expression God uses to tell us that our sins are gone forever.

8. *He has put our sins as far away from us as the east is from the west.* Let New York represent the east and San Francisco the west and you have just a slight idea of how far your sins have been removed by a great God.

9. *He has put our sins behind His back.* Here we are given the idea that God will never look upon our sins again, for He has put them behind His back for all eternity.

And so the Bible tells us that God does a complete job in doing away with our sins. Once you have come to Christ and laid your sins at His feet, looking up to Him for salvation, you can know that your sins are gone — gone forever.

A man came one day and gave a lecture to a group of coal miners in England. He said that the Bible was a collection of myths and fables, that God did not exist, that Christ was a figment of the imagination, and that Christianity was a hoax. At the close of the lecture a miner stood before the group and said, "I am an uneducated man. I am so ignorant that I don't know the meaning of the word 'myth.' But I know this. There was a time when the saloons got all of my money, a time when I would go home and beat my wife and children. Then one day I heard a preacher as he told me the story of Jesus and His power to save a man from sin and the drink habit. I called upon Him to save me and He did. Now I drink no more, my wife and children have what they need and we have a happy home. Can you explain that?" And the lecturer could say no more.

Every saved person is a miracle of God's grace. We are sitting pretty because of what God has done about our sins. You can't beat that.

> How firm a foundation, ye saints of the Lord,
> Is laid for your faith in His excellent Word!
> What more can He say than to you He hath said,
> To you, who for refuge to Jesus have fled?

II. Christians Are Sitting Pretty Because They Have the Holy Spirit as a Daily Companion

Jesus said that the Holy Spirit would come down to abide with us forever. And the moment we trust Christ as Saviour and Lord He comes to live in our hearts. Now what does He do for us?

1. *The Holy Spirit brings daily conviction.* As radar finds the enemy and points him out, so does the Holy Spirit locate sin in us and point it out to us. When a person be-

comes a Christian the old damning sin is gone, although he is still subject to temptation. He will sin in some way every day, in deed or thought or word. You can't lie down to sleep at night and say, "I have not sinned today." In some way you have fallen short of the glory of God.

And here is where the Holy Spirit, dwelling in the Christian, goes to work. He will say, "Here is where you sinned today. Here is the thing that ought not to be in your life." Then the child of God will want to confess his sin, asking God for forgiveness. Of course a person can stifle and silence the voice of the Spirit. He can crowd his heart with so many worldly things that he cannot hear that voice. But when the Christian listens, the Holy Spirit will bring conviction and cause him to want to be rid of his sin.

2. *The Holy Spirit brings daily cleansing.* As the physical body needs daily cleansing, so does the spiritual life. Jesus illustrated this truth when He washed the disciples' feet. Their bodies were clean, but they had been walking the dusty roads, so their feet needed cleansing. When a person comes to Christ, he is cleansed from the old Adamic sin which had doomed him to death. But other sins are bound to come in every day and he needs to be cleansed from these sins.

That cleansing comes through the Holy Spirit when we confess our sins to God. "If we confess our sins, he is faithful and just to forgive us our sins, and to cleanse us from all unrighteousness" (I John 1:9). Every day we ought to report to God and say, "Lord, You saved me, but here is something wrong which crept in today. The Holy Spirit has revealed it to me. Now cleanse me, Lord, so that there shall be nothing between Thee and me." And the Holy Spirit will then dip us in the cleansing blood and make us clean again.

3. *The Holy Spirit guides us each day.* The Bible says,

"I will guide thee with mine eye" (Psalm 32:8). A certain preacher and his family were to entertain a prominent woman at a dinner party. The preacher instructed his teen-age son to sit next to the woman and supply all of her needs. He told the boy that he would guide him with his eye. If the woman's water glass needed filling, the preacher would look at the water pitcher and then at the empty glass, and then the boy would fill the glass. If the preacher saw that the woman needed salt and pepper, he would look at the salt and pepper and then at the woman's plate and the boy would know what to do.

This arrangement worked well. Throughout the meal the father guided his son with his eye, without saying a word to him. So as we look up to the Holy Spirit, He guides us with His eye.

4. *The Holy Spirit comforts us in time of sorrow.* I have conducted many funerals. I have seen many people in the hour of sorrow. Some of them were simply torn to pieces, they knew not where to turn for comfort. But others, who had sorrows just as deep, had the peace of God written upon their faces and comfort filled their hearts. What caused the difference? Some of them knew not the Lord, while others knew Him personally. They looked up into His face and were comforted by the Holy Spirit.

In Thessalonica many Christians were losing their loved ones in death. Their sorrow was great. Paul said to them, "You are not to sorrow like others which have no hope." Then he went on to tell them that since they were Christians they had hope in Christ. He would one day come back and reunite them with their loved ones. So when we have sorrow the Holy Spirit whispers, "Let not your heart be troubled. You have lost them just for a while. You will see them again some day. Just lean on Me and I will comfort you."

Yes, we are sitting pretty because of what God has

done with our sins. We are sitting pretty because we have the Holy Spirit as a daily companion. Now one other thought.

III. We Are Sitting Pretty Because of What God Will Do About Our Future

There is an old song which says, "I'm so glad that trouble doesn't last always." This is a joyful truth. We don't have to live here forever in this vale of tears. It's a good thing that God lets us grow old. Suppose that we stopped growing at twenty and remained strong and young. Maybe we would want to stay on here forever. But when we get to be seventy or eighty and the body begins to fall apart, we say, "I'm ready now. I'm ready to go out, and get the new body God has promised me."

Someone has declared that the greatest sentence in the English language is, "This, too, shall pass away." So as we struggle down the highway of life, we can say about all of our troubles, "One day all of this will pass away and I shall be in the land of fadeless day, where God shall wipe away all of my tears."

When Jesus said, "I go to prepare a place for you, where you can live forever," He didn't go out to do a shoddy job. He has a perfect heaven waiting for us, where we shall live in perfect bodies throughout a perfect eternity.

John said, "It doth not yet appear what we shall be." He is simply saying that we are going to be different. The change will be so wonderful that our finite minds cannot possibly conceive of it. But we do know one thing. We shall be like Jesus.

1. *We shall be like Him in holiness.* The Lord asked Solomon to choose any gift and it would be his. He chose wisdom and God made him the wisest man on earth. But his wisdom didn't save him from sin. If he had chosen

holiness, surely his life would have been different. In heaven we will have no sin. We will be holy, even as Christ is holy.

2. *We shall be like Him in love.* We don't love everyone, but God does. However, in heaven we shall love everyone and they will love us, because we shall all be like Jesus.

3. *We shall be like Him mentally.* Lord Tennyson was a cripple. One day he took a walk with a friend. Tennyson walked very slowly and soon his friend was fifty yards in front of him. This friend heard a cry from Tennyson and went back to find him on his knees, looking at a beautiful water flower growing in a shallow pool. "What a great imagination God has," exclaimed Tennyson. In that day we shall have His mentality and His imagination. All of the mysteries of the universe and all of the riddles of life will be clear in the day when we become like Him.

4. *We shall be like Him physically.* We are told that in the twinkling of an eye we shall be changed into His own glorious likeness. In His resurrection body He was not subject to any laws of gravity or physics. He could pass through closed doors and transcend any space. Often, when we have a trip of a thousand miles facing us, we say, "I wish I could just wish myself there." Well, in that day if we are on one side of heaven and want to go to the other side, we can do it in a split second of time.

God is a God of perfection. He never leaves anything undone. He takes care of the past by providing us with a Saviour and forgiving our sins. He takes care of the present by sending the Holy Spirit to be our daily companion. He takes care of the future by providing a wonderful home for us.

When Billy Graham was in Africa he visited a tiny village to preach to a small band of Christians. All of them had been severely persecuted. Their homes had been burned, their possessions had been taken away, some of their loved ones had been killed by the Moslem authorities. They worshiped in a little hut about ten by twelve feet in size. Some of them had walked a dozen miles to hear the great evangelist. When Billy Graham arrived he was treated with the greatest respect. As he looked about him, he said that he could see the marks of suffering on the faces of many of them. And the first song they sang was, "There'll be no dark valley when Jesus comes."

Oh, my friends, that is Christianity. Give yourself to Jesus. He will wash away your sins. He will walk down the pathway of life with you. And though suffering and sorrow may be your lot, He will see you through every dark valley and bring you at last to the land that is fairer than day.

3

Put a Ring on His Finger
Luke 15:22

Jesus was the greatest storyteller who ever lived. In the fifteenth chapter of Luke He is at His best. He tells of a boy who left home and wandered off into the far country. Over there he got in with the wrong crowd. He spent his days and nights in riotous living and revelry. But his money soon gave out, he went down and down, his fairweather friends all forsook him. Finally he lands in a hogpen, where it was his duty to feed the swine.

Then one day he came to himself. He decided to go home. He thought he could slip into the house unnoticed, then he would ask his father to let him be just another hired servant. Even that would be better than feeding pigs in a foreign land. But he didn't figure on the great love of his father. That dear man was out in front of the house, watching, waiting, hoping for the return of his son. And when he saw his son coming down the road he ran to meet him. He threw his arms around the boy and kissed him. The boy began to confess his sins, but the father stopped him. He turned to the servants and said, "Bring the best robe and put it on my boy. Bring a ring for his finger and shoes for his feet. Then kill the fatted calf and let's have a feast. My son, who was dead, is alive again. He was lost, but now he is found."

Now the father puts his arm around the boy's shoulders and they go into the house together. No more sin in the far country, no more feeding swine, no more eating husks, no more blistered feet on the highway. All sins have been forgiven and the son is home at last. That's the way God receives a sinner. The sinner comes in rags and God gives him a robe of righteousness. He comes as a poor, lost, hell-bent sinner and God forgives him, adopts him into the family of heaven and gives him the best of all things in two worlds.

Now in the story we hear the father saying, "Put a ring on his finger." Rings are wonderful things. Some are of gold, some of pearl, some of rubies, or diamonds. There is the birthday ring, the engagement ring, the wedding ring. But, symbolically, the best ring of all is ours when we come to Christ and put our faith in Him. Let us think of three rings which come to us when we place our faith and trust in the Lord Jesus Christ.

I. The Ring of Adoption

When we come to Christ we are adopted into God's family. We were born in sin and we belong to Satan's family. But when we are converted God takes us over and adopts us into His family.

1. *We have different clothes when God adopts us.* The prodigal's old clothes were thrown away and he received a new robe. When a child is adopted by a family, they provide new clothes for him. It is the same way with us when we are saved. Our outward apparel may not be changed, but when a man becomes a real Christian, he sheds the old clothes of sin and selfishness and worldliness. He puts on the new clothes of God's righteousness, the new clothes of a good life and a right attitude.

Businessmen keep a chart in their offices. These charts show the changing, the ups and downs of business conditions. The chart of a man's life also shows his ups and downs. But his life ought to be altogether changed when

Put a Ring on His Finger 33

he comes to Christ. First, there is the low line, depicting his life before he was saved. Then the line reaches a peak the moment he trusts Jesus. From that time on the line should be climbing upward, onward, Godward. Oh, the Christian is to take off the garments of this world and be clothed in the beautiful garments of the Spirit.

2. *We have different parents when God adopts us.* When an earthly couple adopts a child, one who is not his father becomes his father and one who is not his mother becomes his mother. The Bible tells us that Satan is the sinner's father, but when we come to Christ God becomes our Father. Then we can say, "Our Father who art in heaven."

Great it would be to be the son of the president or the son of some great and prominent and wealthy man. Great it would be to be the child of royal parents. But how much more wonderful to be able to say, "God is my Father since I've been adopted into His family."

A sixteen year old girl knelt to pray, and in her usual way she began with "Our Father." He meant very little to her. But then one day she found Christ as her Saviour. Her prayer was changed. She began, "My Father," and a flood of joy rolled over her. She came to realize that He was not merely the Father of all men in a creative sense, but her own Father through redemption.

3. *We have different homes when God adopts us.* Many children have been taken out of homes of poverty and adopted into homes of luxury and comfort. So when God adopts us, when we become real Christians, our homes are remade.

Gypsy Smith was holding a meeting one time and a little girl came up and gave him a box of candy. "Why do you give me this candy?" he asked. She said, "My father used to drink. He would come home and mistreat mother and us children. He never brought home the things we needed. But one night he came to hear you preach and he found Christ as His Saviour. Now we have a wonderful home. He brings us all the nice things we need. I want to give you this candy in appreciation of all you did for us in leading daddy to Christ." Yes, when you let Jesus come into your home it makes all the difference in the world.

4. *We have different inheritances when God adopts us.* Not poverty, but riches. Not rags, but robes. What is the sinner's inheritance? Judgment and hell. What is the Christian's inheritance? We become heirs of God and joint heirs with the Lord Jesus Christ. Everything good awaits the child of God.

Here is a room in a fine home in the early morn. One man comes in and dusts the furniture, so we know that he is a servant. Another man looks around at the pictures on the wall and the books on the shelf. He selects a book and sits down and leafs through its pages. We know he is a guest in the home. Then a boy comes in. He looks through the mail on the table and when another man comes into the room he rushes into his arms, calling him "Father." We know that he is the son. What a difference! So in God's family we are more than servants, more than guests, we are His children. Jesus is our Elder Brother and we are the heirs of God.

Yes, here is the ring of adoption. No matter how black our sin, no matter how far we have gone from God, when we come in repentance and faith to Christ, He puts the ring of adoption on our finger, and all of heaven and earth knows we have been adopted. "As many as received him, to them gave he the power to become the sons of God" (John 1:12).

II. The Ring of Marriage

In Hosea 2:19 we read, "I will betroth thee unto me

for ever." God is saying here that we are joined to Him forever.

1. *When we are saved we become one with Christ.* In the marriage ceremony the groom slips a ring on the bride's finger and the preacher says that the twain have become one flesh. So at the foot of the cross, when we accept Jesus, we become as one.

There is the ring on the bride's finger. Trouble and hard times come to the home. The young couple may have to sell the picture or the piano, but never the ring. It has a meaning nothing else can have. Then one sad day the husband passes away. As the wife looks at the ring, tears fill her eyes and sweet memories flood her heart. She recalls that day when he put the ring on her finger and they became one.

Oh, when Christ puts that ring on you, you and He become one in love and hope and affection. Let's never forget that day when Jesus washed our sins away and we became His very own.

2. *When we are saved we become one with Christ forever.* It's a permanent transaction. A union is formed which nothing on earth or in heaven or hell can break.

Today many marriages end in divorce. A union which begins in so much love and happiness goes stale and soon another divorce is ground out in the court, another marriage has gone on the rocks. But not so with our marriage to Christ, our union with Him. We are joined to Him forever. The life He gives us is everlasting.

He never turns His back upon us and we should never turn our backs upon Him. Many years ago a Scottish girl was called on to denounce Christ. When she refused to do so, they took her out into the ocean some distance and tied her to a stake. They expected that when the tide came in, she would renounce her faith. The water soon came up to her waist, then to her breast, then to her neck. Finally the water closed over her head and she drowned shouting the praises of her Saviour.

The soul that on Jesus has leaned for salvation can never be lost, can never be separated from Christ. "I give unto them eternal life; and they shall never perish, neither shall any man pluck them out of my hand. My Father, which gave them me, is greater than all; and no man is able to pluck them out of my Father's hand" (John 10: 28, 29). Romans 8:38, 39 says, "For I am persuaded, that neither death, nor life, nor angels, nor principalities, nor powers, nor things present, nor things to come, Nor height, nor depth, nor any other creature, shall be able to separate us from the love of God, which is in Christ Jesus our Lord."

The seas may dry up, the mountains may crumble, the sun may melt away, but Christ will never desert us. Thank God, when He saves He saves forever. We are bound to Him with a chain that can never be broken. We are His and He is ours, forever and forever.

III. THE RING OF FESTIVITY

The most glorious moment of life is that moment when we become joined to Christ. Then the ring of festivity is placed upon us and we rejoice in Christ our Saviour. Some people think that the religion of Christ robs one of all pleasure, but just the opposite is true. Our joy is multiplied a thousand fold. The finest freedom, the largest liberty, the greatest happiness, all are found in Christ. Let us look at some of the good things that are ours in Him.

1. *Our sins are forgiven.* It is good to remember that God bundles up all of our sins and throws them into the sea of His forgetfulness, where they can never rise again. If our sins are not forgiven, if they stand between us and God, we have no right to smile or sing. Our condition is a miserable one.

A Hindu native came to a missionary and said, "Give

me some of that medicine which makes the face shine." The missionary asked, "What do you mean?" The native replied, "I notice that your Christians have shining faces, and I want some of that medicine." Yes, we do have that medicine — the medicine of sins forgiven. This is enough to make anyone shout for joy.

2. *Our burdens are lighter.* I do not mean that our burdens are fewer, but we have help in our Elder Brother, Jesus.

A boy became involved in a scrap with a boy who was much bigger than he was. Someone asked him, "Aren't you afraid?" And he replied, "No, you see my older brother is just around the corner." I say to you, that in the battles of life, Jesus is not around the corner, He is right by your side.

3. *Our fellowship is sweeter.* Two Christians were talking and one of them said, "It's a good thing to be saved." The other said, "There is something grander than that." "What can be grander than that?" asked the first man. And the other replied, "The companionship of the Man who saved you." Yes, on every road we travel, He is there.

4. *Our future is brighter.* Oh, the Christian's future is indeed brighter than the sun. One day all of our uncertainties will change to glorious assurance. On the way home you may be in an accident and your life may be snuffed out. But that will be all right. If you are a Christian you'll walk the golden streets of the celestial city, where congregations never break up and where Sabbaths never end.

A lingering disease may lay you low. You may waste away slowly until the end. But if you are a Christian you need have no fear. Your real self will rise up from that bed and you'll stand by the side of your Saviour, in a land where weeping and toiling shall be no more.

On a bitter, cold morning a man said to a newsboy, "Certainly is a cold morning, isn't it?" But the boy said, "Yes, but by and by, think of that!" We are in a cold world. Sorrow and trouble surround us. But think of the sweet by and by, think of how wonderful it's going to be.

When the labors of the week are over, we say, "Tomorrow is my day of rest." But let me tell you something more pleasant than that. At the end of the life it will be sweet to say, "My work is over and I am going home to enjoy an everlasting rest."

Some of you are not far from heaven. Just a few more sermons, a few more songs, a few more tears and toils, and your time will come. Oh, glorious day! Say, friend, are you on the way? Or are you out in the far country of sin? Come and let Jesus put a ring on your finger. This world has nothing to satisfy you. Come to Him.

Let me draw you a picture of a scene at the gates of heaven. A group comes up from the earth and the doorkeeper asks for the password. "Password," they say, "we know no password. But we were great upon the earth and we expect to be great in heaven." Then they hear the voice of the Saviour just beyond the gate as He says, "I never knew you." And they are turned away.

Another group comes up and they are asked for the password. "We have no password," they say. "But on the earth we did noble things. We endowed colleges, we built hospitals, we helped the poor." And again the voice of the Lord is heard as He says, "Depart from Me. No man enters heaven through the works of the flesh." And they are turned away.

Then a third group comes and they are asked for the password. They say, "We wandered far away from God. We deserved to die. But we heard the voice of Jesus calling us, so we put all our trust in Him. We come in His Name, the Name of the Lord Jesus Christ."

Then the gatekeeper cries out, "That's the password. Jesus is the password to heaven. Lift up your heads, ye everlasting gates, and let the redeemed of the Lord enter in." And all the hosts of heaven sing and all the bells of heaven ring as the children of the King walk into heaven and into the presence of their Lord.

My friend, the only way to get into heaven and all of its joy is through the Lord Jesus Christ. Have you made Him your personal Saviour?

4

Jesus Calls Us
John 21:20-25

Some years ago a man spoke in the chapel of one of our great universities. He offered good positions to the students gathered there. Good pay, pleasant working conditions, future security, all were promised to these men. But the response to the offer was negligible. Very few men seemed to be interested. But on another day a grizzled missionary veteran spoke to that same group. He did not paint a beautiful picture. He told of the hardships and dangers awaiting anyone who would accept his challenge to follow Christ on a difficult frontier. Although he could promise only hardships and suffering, there was a ready response to his challenge. A host of young men expressed their willingness to undertake this difficult mission for Christ.

The call of Christ is never a call to the easy life. Yet a life of service to Christ has compensations offered by no other life. We can always count on His presence along the way and His blessing and reward at the end of the way. The man who follows the call of the world will have no Great Friend by his side, and no one to meet him at the end of life and usher him into a glorious eternity.

In our text we see Jesus at the end of His earthly stay. His marvelous life has been lived and His sacrifice for us on Calvary has been made. He has burst the bonds of death and the grave and has come back to life again. Now the time is up and He is going back to heaven to occupy His place in glory. We hear Him talking to Simon Peter and giving him instructions for his life. Then Peter pointed to John and said, "What about John? What is he going to do?" And Jesus answered, "What is that to thee? Follow thou me." This is what He says to all of us. No matter what anyone else says or does, we are to follow Jesus. Others may criticize, others may fall by the wayside, others may question our motives, but we must follow Jesus and obey His every command, regardless.

The world is full of calls, the call to make money, the call to get an education, the call to enjoy cultural advantages, the call to serve one's country, the call to please loved ones, the call to have a big time in life. There is the call of the heart and the call of the flesh. But the greatest, sweetest, clearest call of all is the call of Jesus, "Follow thou me."

I. Jesus Calls Us to Leave all Sin

When a group of archaeologists dug into ruins of ancient Babylon, they found that every brick had upon it the stamp of the king. But upon one brick they found the print of a dog's foot. Evidently a dog had stepped upon the brick while it was still soft and his footprint now covered the king's stamp. God has His stamp upon His children, but often we allow sin to cover the image of the Lord. We want others to see Jesus in us but, alas, His image is often marred by our sin.

It may be that you are not guilty of gross, open sin, but Jesus warns us against the sins of the spirit, the sins of a bad disposition and a wrong attitude. These sins are not always visible to the naked eye, but they are sometimes more hurtful than the sins of the flesh. We often recognize the sins of the flesh and repent of them, while we harbor these other sins in our hearts and let them ruin our spiritual lives and testimony.

In the sixth chapter of Proverbs God mentions seven things that He hates:

(1) *"A proud look."* Some people are proud of their money, their position, their education, and some are even proud of their religion. God despises such an attitude. The Pharisee in the Temple stood where everyone could see him and hear him as he prayed, "Lord, I thank thee that I am not as other men." We have too many people like that today. God is never pleased with such an attitude.

(2) *"A lying tongue."* Oh, what damage a lying tongue can do. Some people have become so saturated with the lying habit that they lie when the truth would be easier to tell and would benefit them much more.

(3) *"Hands that shed innocent blood."* Of course murder is a sin and not many Christians are guilty of it. But we are also guilty when we do things that make the hearts of others to bleed.

(4) *"Wicked imaginations."* This is where sin starts. Only two people can dwell in you at one time, you and God, or you and Satan. Let God dwell in you and from your imaginations will come good words and noble deeds. But let Satan dwell in your heart and only wicked things will come from your life.

(5) *"Feet swift in running to mischief."* Often we crawl to do good deeds, but we run when we have a chance to hurt someone.

(6) *"A false witness that speaketh lies."* We hear a bit of gossip about someone. We don't bother to check on it, but we get someone's reputation under our feet and we grind it to pieces. When we hear something that would hurt someone, we ought to ask God the question, "Should I repeat this to someone else?" And I am sure you know what His answer would be.

(7) *"He that sows discord among brethren."* This is wickedness in the highest degree. How often have we seen

the sweet fellowship in a church broken up by one whose delight was to promote discord. Some people just can't stand for peace and harmony to reign. Their greatest joy is found in stirring up strife. These people never do anything useful. They have no time or inclination to serve God and help others. They simply want to hurt someone. God hates this kind of thing.

Sin of any kind is displeasing to God. Every sin is a slap in the Saviour's face, every sin crucifies Him afresh. God calls on you to get rid of the sin in your life. Why not say today, "Lord, I am sorry that I have sinned against Thee. Forgive me and help me to live so that others will see Thy image in me. Oh, let there be nothing between me and Thee."

II. Jesus Calls Us to Serve Him Better

Peter had served Jesus in a way, but when the testing time came he failed the Lord. Now Jesus recalls him. "Follow Me," He said. After this Peter's life is altogether different. No more does he live in the shallows of life and for this world only. Every day is spent in the service of Christ. Maybe you've been content just to be a church member. That is not enough. Jesus calls you to leave your indifference and give your best to Him.

We never know how much depends on the way we serve Christ. I am thinking of a fine couple I knew in past days. They were church members, but just nominal Christians. I begged them, for the sake of their son if for nothing else, to give of their best to the Master. But they went their indifferent way, putting all else before Christ. Their son grew up to be almost an infidel and to break their hearts. You may say that your service to Christ means very little, but the destiny of your best beloved may depend upon it.

The happiness of a Christian depends upon the way he

serves the Saviour. After having served Him faithfully, you can never find happiness in living any other way. The King's service is so satisfying that, once you engage in it, you can never find joy in any other kind of life.

I go up and down the streets of the city, I enter into many homes. People talk to me about their relationship to God and the church. They tell me of how they once served Christ and of the joy which was theirs. But now they are out of the church and out of touch with God. They are living useless lives and they are miserable. Are you one of them? Listen, yonder on the throne is One who loved you. He left heaven's glory for you, He died on the cross for you, He rose from the grave for you, He is daily interceding for you.

He says to you, "Don't be content to live only for self. Come with Me. Give up your indifference and neglect. Let's go out together to help men and glorify God. Only then can you find true happiness and real satisfaction."

III. JESUS CALLS US TO A DEEPER PRAYER LIFE

How deep is your prayer life? Some people never pray. Others pray once in a while when they get into some sort of trouble. Some are so busy that they offer only a sentence to God every day. But some live close to God and talk to Him often as to a friend.

The song says, "Oh, what peace we often forfeit. . . . All because we do not carry everything to God in prayer." Peace is certainly what we need these days. We live in such a restless world, our hearts are so often torn with trouble. Most of us know what it is to carry a heavy burden, to lie awake at night, to wet our pillows with our tears. We need peace more than anything else and prayer is the surest way to find it. Let's not try to carry our burdens alone. Let's take them to Jesus in prayer.

A minister knelt by the bedside of one of his sick

members and offered a prayer. Then she said, "Pastor, let me pray for you," and she did. Then she said, "For the ten years that you have been my pastor I have prayed for you every morning and every night." We ought to pray for others. It is not enough just to pray for ourselves. We ought to engage daily in intercessory prayer, remembering those who need the Lord's help.

We also need to learn to pray another type of prayer. Jesus said that we are to pray for those who despitefully use us. We can learn a great lesson right here. Our prayers may not change our enemies, but they will certainly change us. Prayer will help us get the hatred out of our own hearts and to look upon all men in the right way.

Jesus was treated far worse than we have been treated, yet He could pray, "Father, forgive them; for they know not what they do" (Luke 23:34). If His spirit lives in us we can fall on our knees and say, "Lord, here is one who has hurt me. He has said and done things against me. But Lord, bless him and help me to hold nothing against him. Help me treat him in such a way as to remind him of Jesus." Oh, we have so many problems in life. We can't work them out alone, so let us take them to Him in prayer.

IV. Jesus Calls Us to Read the Bible More

I have seen lives of Christians changed by the magic power of the Word of God. Let a man get into the Bible and let the Bible get in him and a change is bound to come. He will find himself putting aside those things which the Bible condemns, and he will try to conform his life to its teachings. But many of our people never read the Bible. They never seek the authority of the Word, but lean on their own understanding. They never apply the Bible to their lives, their homes, their business. Consequently their lives never become the sweet, useful, consecrated lives they might become.

A certain emperor commissioned an artist to paint his portrait. Now this emperor had a wart on his face of which he was ashamed. When the portrait was finished the artist had drawn a striking likeness of the emperor, including the wart. But when the portrait was presented to the emperor he flew into a rage. He said to the artist, "You know I am embarrassed by that wart. Why did you include it in the picture?" And the artist replied, "Sire, I painted you as you are and not as you would like to be."

Now that's why some men do not read the Bible. It points out their sins and their shortcomings. It paints them as they are and not as they would like to be. Three things we should do about the Bible. We should love it, learn it and live it.

V. Jesus Calls Us to Trust Him More Implicitly

You may say, "I have trusted Him for my salvation. I have turned my life, my soul, my all over to Him for time and eternity." Yes, you have trusted Him to save your soul, you expect Him to take you to heaven at the end of the way. But what about today? If He is able to save your soul, isn't He able to carry your burdens? Yet we do not fully trust Him. When trouble or sorrow come we go all to pieces. Yet the great Saviour wants us to bring every burden to Him.

A man left the hospital after surgery and a long season of recuperation. A good friend walked by his side. When they came to the steps of his home the man's strength had just about given out. The friend said to him, "Lean on me." And soon they were safely up the steps. You and I do not have the strength to climb the steps of life alone, so our Great Friend, the Lord Jesus, says, "Lean on Me. Put all your weight on Me. And we'll make the journey with your hands placed in Mine." As we lean on Him we climb the steps toward heaven hand in hand.

The song says, "The arm of flesh will fail you, you dare not trust your own." How true that is. No one can help you like Jesus. He says, "I will never leave you nor forsake you" (Hebrews 13:5). He says, "I will be with you unto the end of the way." He says, "Commit thy way unto the LORD; trust also in him; and he shall bring it to pass" (Psalm 37:5).

Christians ought to trust Jesus implicitly and then the world would see the reality of their religion. A gentle old lady walked into an elevator in the back part of a store. "You don't have much sunshine back here, do you?" she said to the operator, who answered, "Only when people like you bring it." Christ's people ought to carry sunshine everywhere. If we are trusting Him implicitly our lives can be like rays of sunshine that brighten the day for those in darkness.

VI. Jesus Calls Us to Witness More Consistently

He said, "Ye are my witnesses" (Isaiah 43:10). Are you serving as His witness? Is anyone a follower of Christ because of your witness to them?

A certain woman who was a member of my church lived next door to a young couple, neither of whom knew Christ. Soon a baby was born to this couple, but after a few days of life, the little thing passed away. This dear Christian woman went over and did everything in her power for that young couple in their time of sorrow. They were able to see Jesus in what she did and what she said. Before long this young couple came to church and found Christ as their Saviour. Later on they gave their testimony, saying, "It was because of this dear woman's interest in us that we came to church and were saved."

We may not be able to make a rousing speech or give a glowing testimony, but the main thing is to show people that we are interested and want to see them saved.

VII. Jesus Calls Us to Greater Faithfulness

We hurt ourselves and others when we are not faithful. A young woman was saved years ago under my ministry. Some years later I held a meeting in another state and came in contact with her again. She was married and had a baby girl. But she was living outside of the church and away from God. I tried to win her husband to the Saviour but was unsuccessful. I believe that if the wife had been living a faithful, consistent Christian life, the husband would have felt the need of becoming a Christian. Yes, we hurt ourselves and others when we fail to live rightly for Christ.

But we help others when we are faithful. Two men were talking together one day when another man passed by. One of the men said, "That man's life slew my infidelity." Every man has an influence. A Christian influence is a helpful thing.

On the Junaluska Assembly grounds in North Carolina a cross has been erected upon a high hill. At night it can be seen plainly as a spotlight plays its beams upon it. Jesus our Saviour died upon a cross upon another hill. But it takes our faithful lives to make men see that cross. Our faithfulness calls attention to that cross and the Saviour who gave His life there for us all.

A Jewess in New York City accepted Jesus Christ as her personal Saviour. Her family did everything in their power to influence her to give up her new-found faith. They took her on a trip to Europe, they offered her anything she wanted if she would only deny Christ. But she remained steadfast and radiant in her love for Christ. Finally her parents gave a dinner in her honor and invited all of their friends. Her father stood at the head of the table and said to the guests, "We have invited you here for a special reason. Our daughter has chosen to follow the despised Nazarene. Tonight she must make her final decision. She must give up Jesus or leave our house forever."

The stunned girl said nothing for a moment. Then she went over to the piano and played and sang, "Jesus, I my cross have taken, all to leave and follow Thee." After that she went to her room, changed her dress, packed her clothes, and left her parents' home forever. She was willing to make a supreme sacrifice to follow Jesus. Are we willing to pay the price?

I call you today to stand by the cross and say, "I will not live any longer for my own comfort and pleasure and satisfaction. I will live for Christ and not the world. I will tear all sin out of my life and live faithfully for Jesus." Will you do it?

5

Lost Horizons
Luke 15:8-10

Some years ago James Hilton wrote a book with the title, *Lost Horizons*. In this book he tells of a certain Englishman who was taken off a plane in the mountains of Asia and carried to a place called Shangri-La. Shangri-La was a beautiful and wonderful place. Everyone there was happy and healthy. They had all they needed and they never grew old. This man stayed in Shangri-La for a year and then returned to England. But he was not happy, so he made his way back to Shangri-La and to the rich and happy life he had enjoyed there. He found his happiness where he had left it.

This is true in every walk of life. We usually find the good things of life just where we lost them. Jesus, in one of His marvelous stories, tells us of a woman who had a band of ten silver coins. One day she lost one of the coins. So she lighted a candle and swept the floor carefully until she found the lost coin. Then she called in her friends and neighbors to rejoice with her.

In these days of stress and strain and tension, some of us have lost our spiritual values. We are not living as close to God as once we did. Our faith is often of a lukewarm variety and God seems afar off. Our Christianity doesn't have the warm glow of former days. We have lost some things, some very valuable and worthwhile things. Surely we would like to recover them. I hope that in this message I can help you to find them.

II. WHAT ARE SOME OF THE SPIRITUAL VALUES WE HAVE LOST?

1. *We have lost the consciousness of God's nearness*. Do you remember how very near you felt to Him right after your conversion? You felt that He was by your side. You could hardly wait until time to go to church, where you would hear more about Him. Those were glorious days. A young man who worked in a machine shop was saved in the church where I ministered. A little later I went out to the machine shop to visit him. He stopped his machine and said to me, "Pastor, life for me is certainly wonderful now. I get along with the boss better than ever. The work doesn't seem so monotonous and the hours don't seem nearly so long." What had happened to him? The boss was just as grouchy as ever. The work was just as tedious and the hours were just as long. But the man was different on the inside. Christ had made the difference.

Yes, life takes on a new and wonderful meaning when Christ comes in. But the days go by and we get far away from Him. We lose the sense of His presence. Now He hasn't moved away, we have.

Thomas lost this consciousness. He doubted that Christ had risen from the grave. But Jesus came to him one glorious Sunday and said, "Thomas, reach hither thy finger and behold my hands; and reach hither thy hand, and thrust it into my side: and be not faithless, but believing" (John 20:26). And dear old doubting Thomas cried out, "My Lord, and my God" (verse 27). But some of us reach out to Him these days and He doesn't seem to be there. We have lost the consciousness of His presence.

2. *We have lost the joy of His salvation*. There is a joy in the salvation that Jesus gives. Do you remember when they sang,

> Just as I am, without one plea,
> But that Thy blood was shed for me,

> And that Thou bidd'st me come to Thee,
> O Lamb of God, I come! I come.

Your heart was stirred, you were convicted of sin, your spirit was moved and tears filled your eyes. You walked down the aisle and surrendered your all to Jesus. Then the joy bells rang in your soul and you felt like singing:

> O happy day that fixed my choice
> On Thee, my Savior and my God!
> Well might this glowing heart rejoice,
> And tell its raptures all abroad.

You were very happy in Christ in the days that followed. You rejoiced that He had reached down and saved you from your sin and set your feet upon the road that leads to heaven. But the days came and went and you became involved in other things. Now you get no thrill out of remembering that you are a child of God. It doesn't cheer you to think of your relationship to Him.

After David's great sin he cried out, "Restore unto me the joy of thy salvation" (Psalm 51:12). He hadn't lost salvation, but the joy of it. There are many people in our churches who have no spiritual joy. Their theme song should be, "Where is the joy that once I knew, when first I met the Lord?" Yes, many of us have lost the joy of salvation, the radiance of our religion.

3. *We have lost the sweetness of Christian fellowship.* The Psalmist said, "I was glad when they said unto me, Let us go into the house of the Lord" (Psalm 122:1). There he had not only touched God, he had also enjoyed the fellowship of kindred spirits.

The same experience was ours in former days. But now some of us have so far lost the sweetness of Christian fellowship that we dodge our fellow Christians.

4. *We have lost the loftiness of our Christian ideals.* Once Christ was our ideal. We held high standards of

right and wrong. Often we would say to ourselves, "I can't do that for I am a Christian." But friends pressed temptation upon us and we finally surrendered, saying, "After all, there is no harm in it."

I know a man who was once a bitter foe of liquor. In a group or just in conversation with one man, he would declare that a Christian should never drink. But there came a time when he fell out with his church and began to drift away from God. He soon succumbed to temptation and began to drink. He had lost his ideals. For many Christians their ideals were once like a great light shining in the heavens, leading toward God. Now those ideals have fallen to the ground and anything goes.

5. *We have lost our power in prayer*. Do you remember the time when you lived so close to God that you talked to Him as your best friend? You daily poured out your heart to Him and kept your life in line with His will. But now you pray only when you are in trouble and forget God the rest of the time. You have lost something. Your prayer life is powerless.

6. *We have lost the joy of Christian service.* Once your greatest joy came as you served the Lord. Then that service became drudgery. You became unfaithful to your tasks and soon you quit the Lord's service altogether. Something went out of your life. You tried other things — clubs, sports, the world. But your heart was still empty. You had lost the joy of Christian service.

II. How Do We Lose These Spiritual Values?

1. *They may be lost through sin.* As a cloud hides the face of the sun, so does sin hide the face of God. You can carry a bit of radium in a box in your pocket. In time it will eat its way through the box, through your clothes and into your flesh.

Sin is like that. It gets into the life, eats its way down

into your heart and destroys your spiritual happiness. You lose your high horizons.

2. *They may be lost through neglect.* Neglect is tragic anywhere. Neglect your business and you will suffer loss. Neglect your health and you will lose it. But it is even more tragic to neglect your spiritual life. First, you quit reading the Bible, then you cease to pray, then you stay away from God's house. Before long your religion will be a dormant thing.

> I walked by the woodland meadows,
>   Where sweet the thrushes sing,
> And found on a bed of mosses
>   A bird with a broken wing.
> I healed its wound — and each morning
>   It sang its old sweet strain;
> But the bird with the broken pinion
>   Ne'er soared so high again.
>
> I found a young life broken
>   By sin's seductive art!
> And touched with a Christ-like pity
>   I took him to my heart.
> He lived with a noble purpose,
>   And struggled, not in vain;
> But the life that sin had stricken
>   Ne'er soared so high again.
>
> But the bird with the broken pinion
>   Kept another from the snare;
> And the life that sin had stricken,
>   Raised another from despair.
> Each loss had some compensation,
>   There is healing for every pain —
> But the bird with the broken pinion
>   Ne'er soars so high again.

Through sin and neglect your spiritual wing may become broken. You lose your power. You are never your highest self again. But you can come back. To some degree you can become useful again.

III. WHERE SHALL WE FIND THESE SPIRITUAL VALUES AGAIN?

1. *We can find God's nearness through implicit trust.* A certain woman had a saying, "Fear not, God lives." Then one day her faith wavered and she began to weep over some difficulty. Her son rebuked her by saying, "Mother, is God dead?" This quickly brought her to her senses. Faith brings God near.

An aged woman boarded a train with a heavy bundle which she kept in her lap. The conductor told her, "Put your burden down. The train can carry both it and you." Do you have troubles? Bring them to Him.

He says, "Come unto me, all ye that labour and are heavy laden, and I will give you rest" (Matthew 11:28). You say, "I have more than I can bear." Well, then, come to Him. Bring Him all your cares. Soon you will feel His arms under you, soon you'll begin to thank Him, soon you'll feel closer to Him than ever. Through implicit faith you are made to feel God's nearness.

2. *We can find the joy of salvation in repentance and confession.* How did David get back the joy of salvation? He repented of his sin, cried out to God, and was forgiven. You can find your joy in the same way. Repentance brings us closer to Christ and the closer we are to Him the happier we will be. So leave the world and come back to Him.

3. *We can find the sweetness of Christian fellowship through faithful church attendance.* Jesus loved the church and gave Himself for it. He meets His people there. When you absent yourself from God's House you rob yourself of one of the richest joys of life. Nothing on earth is sweeter than real Christian fellowship. The Bible says, "We know that we have passed from death unto life, because we love the brethren" (I John 3:14). A Christian will want to meet

with his brethren in sweet communion in the bonds of Christ.

4. *We can find a loftiness of ideals in a Book and in a Person.* The Bible presents two things, principles and a Person. The principles of Christian living are laid down in the Book; the Person, Jesus Christ, is there to help us to live up to these principles.

It is said that Raphael, the great artist, kept a diamond embedded in the upper edge of his easel. Then when his eyes became weary of looking at dull colors, he would look at the diamond and this toned up his vision. Jesus is our jewel. We need often to lift up our eyes from the dull monotony of life and look to Him.

If a person looks down continually his shoulders will soon begin to sag. If he looks up continually he will become more erect. If our thoughts are on a low level our character will bend downward. If our thoughts are lifted up toward Christ our characters will be lifted up.

5. *We can find the power of prayer on our knees.* The Bible says, "Ye have not because ye ask not" (James 4:2). There is power in prayer but we often neglect to take advantage of that power.

A preacher was holding a revival in a certain church. But the atmosphere was as cold as ice. Everything about the services was mechanical — there was no warmth or spiritual power in evidence. He sent a telegram to the chairman of his deacons back home, explaining the situation. The next night the entire situation was changed. The atmosphere seemed to be charged with spiritual power. Something had happened. Souls were saved and lives were transformed. Then a telegram came to the preacher, telling him how his deacons had met an hour before the time for his service, and how they had prayed for that service. And God answered their prayers.

It was August in Africa and the weather was very hot.

A missionary mother was quite ill. Her little daughter heard the doctor say, "She is burning up with fever. We need some ice to save her." But, alas, there was no ice. The little girl said, "Doctor, she must not die. We must find some ice. God has promised to give us what we need. I'm going to pray for some ice." She began to pray and kept on praying. Later in the day a cloud came up, then there was a light rain, then hail began to fall. It was ice from heaven. God had answered and a life was saved.

> Today I received a letter,
> It wasn't so very long,
> But somehow my heart was lighter,
> And filled with a cheery song.
> For I had been burdened and weary —
> And though the words were few,
> They brought untold blessing and comfort:
> "Dear friend, I'm praying for you."

Here are three children in a family. One makes a request of his father in proper language. The second one lisps just a little bit. The third one cannot speak at all, he just stretches out his arms toward his father. Is he refused? No, a big tear and an anxious face plead for him. Not all of us can couch our prayers in the proper language. We are not all acquainted with theological terms. But that doesn't matter, God sees and knows and understands. He will hear us if we but stretch out our hands to Him.

6. *We can find joy in Christian service by returning to the Lord's work.* There is no joy comparable to that which is found in serving the Lord. A Greek sculptor was working on a statue to be placed high up in the temple, where it would never be seen by passers-by. A friend who saw how painstaking the artist was, said, "Why do you waste your time like that? No one will see your statue." The sculptor replied, "I am not wasting my time. The gods will see it." Oh, do your best work for Jesus. If no

one praises you, it will not matter. God will see your work and reward you for it.

Many years ago a great organ recital was to take place at a certain hour, but the man who was to pump the organ became ill. Whereupon a famous composer volunteered to do the pumping. Someone asked him why he was willing to do such menial work and he replied, "I love music so much that nothing I can do for it seems menial." Oh, if we love Jesus, nothing we can do in His service will ever seem menial. We will enjoy the least service we do in His name.

Three wise men were discussing the question, "What is the greatest evil that can befall humanity?" One answered, "Old age oppressed by poverty." Another answered, "Pain without patience." But the third wisely answered, "The couch of death and no good deeds to light the way." That is indeed a great tragedy, to come to the end of the way and look back to see that you have wasted a life that could have been spent in the service of the Saviour.

Have you lost your high horizons? Have you lost these holy things that are so worthwhile? Have you lost the joy and radiance of your religion? Then come back and seek them. You will find Christ waiting to help you as you start the return trip. He has been waiting for some of you for many years. Why not come back today?

The great artist Dore was traveling through Southern Europe when he lost his passport. When he came to the boundary line he was stopped by a government official. He said to the official, "I have lost my passport, but I am Dore, the artist, please let me through." "Oh, no," said the man, "many people represent themselves as some prominent person but we don't let them through." The more that Dore pled, the more stubborn the man became. Finally the official said, "All right, if you are Dore, take this pencil and draw a picture for me." Dore seized the pencil, looked off for a minute at the majestic mountains and peaceful valleys and began to draw. Soon the official burst out, "You may go, I know you are Dore. No other man could draw like that."

Dear friend, look at your life and works. Are you reproducing the life of Christ? Do your works testify of Him? Can people see that you belong to Jesus?

Come back from the far country and walk again with Jesus. That's the best road for you. That's the sweetest road. That's the road filled with the greatest joy. He is waiting to walk with you. Are you ready?

6

The Best Things in Life
James 1:12-17

What are the best things in life? Let us ask six men. One will say that money is the best thing, another will say that education is the best thing, another will say that good health is the best thing. Still another will say that a radiant personality rates high, while another will speak of fame and yet another will say that love surpasses anything.

But all of these things are fleeting, they are temporal, they can fade away in a moment. Not one can guarantee a happy life. The things that God gives are surely the best things in life. James looked around him as he wrote our text and thought upon the good things of life. Then he reasoned that the good things which were his came not of his own efforts, but they came as a gift from God. So he wrote, "Every good gift and every perfect gift is from above, and cometh down from the father of lights" (James 1:17).

A man sought a gift from another man for a worthy Christian cause. The man refused to give anything, so the first man said, "You ought to give generously. Just think of how the Lord has blessed you." And the man replied, "But I was there when it happened." May God deliver us from a man who takes the credit for all that he has. "I worked hard for my wealth," says one man. But if God had not given him the health and intelligence to make money, where would he be?

One day Dwight L. Moody was passing by an insane asylum. A man came to the fence and said to him, "Have you ever stopped to thank God for a sound mind?" Mr. Moody admitted that he had never done so, whereupon the insane man said, "Well, you ought to get down on your knees right now and thank Him." Yes, every blessing that is ours has come to us because God loved us and showered these gifts upon us.

There is a difference between "good" gifts and "perfect" gifts. James distinguishes between them. Maybe he was saying that God's material gifts were "good," while God's spiritual gifts were "perfect." Whatever his meaning, he was telling us that all of our gifts have come to us from a beneficent, all-loving Heavenly Father.

I. The Good Things in Life

1. *Friends.* Someone has said that "a friend is one who knows all about you and still loves you." Another has said that "a friend is one who comes in when all the world goes out." There are not many people who live up to these definitions. A man is fortunate to have two or three real friends in a lifetime. Many people may claim to be his friend, but only the real ones stand by when it costs them something.

When the martyr John Huss was on the way to the stake, an old friend rushed out of the crowd and gave him a hearty handshake, even though he knew it might cost him his life. Huss smiled his appreciation, for he knew the man had risked his life to show his friendship.

Someone asked a prominent person, "What is the secret of your life?" And the answer came back, "I had a friend." Surely many people have reached the pinnacle of fame, fortune and happiness because they had a friend who helped them along the way. We can't have too many real friends. We can't afford to lose even one.

> A friend in need, my neighbor said to me,
> A friend in need is what I mean to be;
> In time of trouble I will come to you,
> And in the hour of need you'll find me true.
>
> I thought a bit and took him by the hand,
> "My friend," said I, "you do not understand
> The inner meaning of that simple rhyme,
> A friend is what the heart needs all the time."

Yes, it is wonderful to have friends, but they are not the best things in life.

2. *The home.* The home is truly one of God's gifts. The garden where man first lived was a home, and at the end of the journey God has prepared a heavenly home for us.

A burglar one night broke into a home and made his way upstairs. His shoes squeaked and made a lot of noise. Suddenly he heard an angry voice from the bedroom and he stopped and stood still. The voice said, "If you don't take off those shoes and come on in, you're going to be in plenty of trouble. It has been raining for three hours and you are ruining my carpet with the mud you're bringing in. Take off those shoes at once." The burglar went down to his pal, the tears shining in his eyes. "I can't rob that home," he said, "it reminds me too much of my own home."

When I say that the home is one of the good things God has given us, I am not thinking of a home like that. I am thinking of the kind that John Howard Payne immortalized when he sang, "Mid pleasures and palaces though we may roam, be it ever so humble there's no place like home." The home is a good thing, but it is not the best thing in life.

3. *Health.* For many years I served in the pastorate. One of my first responsibilities was that of a spiritual ministry to the sick people in hospitals and homes. Stand-

The Best Things in Life

ing by those bedsides, witnessing pain and suffering and heartache, I came to realize more fully the blessing of good health. Our hospitals stay full of those who are ill and in many homes we find people who are afflicted for life.

The statistics tell us that more people die of heart trouble today than from any other disease. Is it because we are living so fast, because we have so many things to worry us? Is it because there is so much strain on these old hearts of ours? Possibly so.

Yet sickness has its blessings for us, if we will only seek them. Don't waste your opportunities when you are ill. It is a time to pray, a time to read the Bible, a time to become better acquainted with God. It is a time to meditate on the goodness of God. It is a time to make a list of those who have been good to you, so that later you can reciprocate. One of our great preachers once said, "Be careful how you suffer." Your attitude during your illness can either deny Christ or glorify Him.

Yes, health is a good thing, but not the best.

4. *Work.* The unemployment situation depresses us all. We are happy when there is work enough to go around. Lowell said, "No man is born into this world whose work is not born with him." If you have a task, if you are happy in your work, be sure to thank God for it daily. It is a great blessing.

A man was buying a stagecoach ticket for a journey over the mountains. The ticket agent told him that there were three classes of tickets, first, second and third. "What is the difference?" asked the man. "You'll find out later," replied the agent. The man, knowing not what to do, purchased a first-class ticket and got on the stage. Later in the day when they came to a steep climb, the driver cried out, "All first-class passengers keep your seats, all second-class passengers get out and walk, all third-class passengers get out and push."

The world needs pushers today. Too many of us are riding free and not doing any worthwhile work. Jesus was a worker. He said, "My father worketh hitherto and I work" (John 5:17). God created the heavens and the earth, never stopping until He had finished the work. Jesus worked as a carpenter, then as a preacher, a teacher, a great Physician. He never rested until they laid Him in Joseph's tomb. And after a while there He rose to work again. The idler, the loafer, is never happy and makes no contribution to society. It is the worker who builds the world.

Work is a good thing, a real blessing, but not the best thing in life.

II. The Best Things in Life

1. *Salvation and the forgiveness of sins.* You may have money, you may have friends, you may have a home, you may have health, you may have a fine family, but all this amounts to nothing if the burden of sin is upon your heart and your soul is lost.

There was a time when the great men of the world were Christians, and they were not ashamed of it. But think of the world's leaders today. God is not considered in their plans. Think of the actors and actresses who are seen on the movie and television screens and who make headlines in our papers. Few of them stand out for Christ. But you don't have to be rich or famous to fall into this category. Thousands of plain, ordinary people are giving all their time and thought and energy to this world, leaving Christ out of their lives. They are missing the best because they are not following Him.

A hotel bellboy in Toledo, Ohio, went to his room to take a nap. Two attorneys came to his room to bring him some good news. When they knocked on the door, the bellboy cried out, "Get away from that door." But they kept knocking, and when he finally opened the door, they told him he had inherited $25,000.

Christ knocks at the door of our hearts and we say, "Get away." But He comes only to bring us the best things in this life and the life to come. He says, "Behold, I stand at the door and knock." But the latch is on the inside. Only you can open the door. He comes to give you a new heart, to take away your sin, to save you eternally. Surely there is nothing better in life than this.

2. *Conscious fellowship with God.* You may walk with the rich and the great, but how much sweeter to walk with God.

When Nansen was seeking the North Pole there came a day when he found his ship in deep water. He tried to measure the depth but his line would not reach the bottom. So he wrote in his diary, giving the length of the line and adding the words, "Deeper than that." The next day he lengthened the line, but with the same result. It would not touch the bottom. For several days this went on and the notation in his dairy was always, "Deeper than that." That is like the love of God. No matter how we measure it, we must always say, "It is deeper than that." And the sweetness of fellowship in that love can never be told by human lips.

A young lady was brokenhearted over the loss of her father. One day she was looking through tearful eyes at his picture, when she caught a glimpse of some words on a wall motto. Only two words were visible. They were, "Thou remainest." These words came like a message from heaven to her soul. Yes, even when we lose the dearest on earth to us, we still have our Best Friend, Jesus, left.

We read about a Friend who "sticketh closer than a brother." That Friend's name is Jesus. Think of your earthly friends. Is there even one to whom you can reveal the secrets of your heart? Can you tell him about the evil things that creep into your mind, knowing that he will understand? No, there's only one Friend like that, Jesus our Saviour. He understands all about us. He knows about our sins and our weaknesses, but He still loves us. We can go to Him with all our sorrows and all our joys. We can share the sweetest fellowship with Him.

3. *A helpful relationship to His church.* This is a mutual relationship. The church is helpful to you. The church and its ministry come to you in the critical and needful hours of life. When you are down, it lifts you up. When you are weak, it lends you strength. When you are sad, it brings you comfort. When you are in the darkness, it leads you to the light.

Think of what life would be like without the influence of the church. It brought you the knowledge of Christ and salvation and heaven. It helped you to bring up your children. It made your city a better place in which to live. It has enriched your life in every way. If you had a choice between giving up your church or giving up some other organization, you would say, "I must keep my church above all else." All other institutions are man-made. The church is the only divine institution on earth.

Then you can be helpful to the church. The other day I saw a long line of cars on a certain street. The car in front was sputtering and choking, holding up all of the other cars. That car was like some people in the church. They complain and criticize and hold up the progress of the entire church. Let's not be like that. Let's get busy and push and help our church in every way possible.

We owe much to the church. We owe it our love, our service, our time, our money, our prayers, our influence and our energy. We must stand up for it and never be silent when others attack it.

4. *The opportunity of helping others.* The man who goes through the world without helping others is infinitely

poor. One of the greatest joys and thrills of life is to know that you have helped someone else. A lady who raised and gave flowers to other people said, "The flowers I give away never fade." The things we do for others will last forever. Service abides always.

A man in Scotland gave a sick eagle its freedom, then stood at a window to watch what would happen. Soon another eagle swooped down to the ground and began to fan the sick eagle with its wings. Then he lifted the sick eagle with his pinions and flew up, up, up into the blue. The sick eagle soon gathered strength, spread his wings and soared away. The healthy eagle brought invigoration down because he came from the upper air. And when we have been living up in the heights near God, we too will be able to help others and lift them up.

5. *The hope of heaven.* You can't go very far without hope. It makes all of life worthwhile. Ulysses S. Grant worked on a farm when he was a young man. As he rode along on a load of wood he was dreaming of his future. He saw himself as a colonel, leading a regiment. He dreamed of being highly honored, applauded by the multitudes, traveling over Europe with a beautiful wife. It seemed foolish for a poor man, riding on a load of wood, to dream like this. But all of his dream came true. Hope causes us to dream of a beautiful, happy, wonderful life. And these hopes will find fruition in heaven, where every dream will come true.

I have been to the seashore and have seen the tracks made there in the sand. I have seen the holes dug by children and all sorts of scars on the beach. Then I have seen the old ocean coming in with a mighty rush, obliterating every scar and smoothing out the sands. That is what heaven is like. Life is full of scars and troubles, but heaven will wash them all away. Every scar and stain will be gone.

God is good to us. He gives us His best, here and hereafter. Because of this our hearts ought to be filled with gratitude. We ought to love Him and serve Him. We ought to show our gratitude by giving Him our very lives.

Pierre Hurlat was the best gunner in the French army. He saved his money and built a home in a certain village. It was a thing of beauty, covered with honeysuckle vines and surrounded by flowers. He looked forward to the time of retirement, when he could go there to live in peace. Then came the Franco-Prussian War and the Germans took over the little village and moved into Pierre's home.

One day Pierre found himself beside his gun, on a hill overlooking that village. The general said to him, "Do you see that cottage?" The cold sweat broke out on Pierre's brow, for he knew the general was pointing to the little home that he loved. "A nest of Germans is in that house. I want you to train your gun on it and destroy it." The obedient soldier aimed his gun with all the skill at his command, there was a roar and the cottage was demolished. "Good work," said the general. But as he looked at Pierre he saw that his face was covered with tears. "What's the matter?" he asked Pierre. "Ah, general," the faithful soldier replied, "that was my own house."

He gave his best for the country he loved. Ought we not to give our best to the One we love, to Jesus Christ our Saviour? He gave His best for us.

7

Heaven's Theme Song
Revelation 5:1-14

Today, as we look around upon the world and all of its troubles and tumult, it seems that the cause of Christ is a losing cause. There are millions who never give Him a thought. There are millions who have never confessed Him as Lord and Saviour. Also, great multitudes are living for the world, the flesh and the devil. Their lives are completely given over to this world and its pleasures and problems.

The international outlook is as dark as the individual outlook. The nations of the world hate and suspect each other and are ready to spring at one another's throats. We don't see any of the "peace on earth" which we so glibly talk about at Christmas time. Neighbors are not loving others as they love themselves. Men are not bowing at the feet of Jesus.

But this is just a part of God's overall picture. These days form only a small part of God's great eternal plan. Everything is moving toward the Great Consummation. There is coming a day when Christ will come in glory and become at last King of kings and Lord of lords. Then every knee will bow and every tongue confess that He is Lord, to the glory of God the Father. This will not happen in this church age and all of our efforts will not bring it to pass. He must come first to remove His people from the earth (I Thess. 4:13-18). Then after a period of tribulation upon the earth, He will come in glory to bring into being His Kingdom upon earth.

In the fifth chapter of Revelation we see a vivid picture of this triumph. John looks upon a majestic scene in heaven. God is "on" His throne, in His hand He holds a book with seven seals. Then an angel cries out, "Who is worthy to open the book, and to loose the seals thereof?" (verse 2). No man in heaven or earth or under the earth is able to open the book. John breaks down and weeps because no one is found worthy to open the book.

Then one of the elders said, "Weep not, the Lion of the tribe of Judah will open the book and loose the seals" (verse 5). John looked up to see a fearsome lion, but instead of a lion he saw a little Lamb, wet with the blood of sacrifice. The Lamb came, took the book and opened the seals one by one. Then all the hosts of heaven began to sing. The song grew in volume until every creature in heaven and earth and under the earth had lifted their voices in a mighty paen of praise. They sang out, "Worthy is the Lamb that was slain to receive power, and riches, and wisdom, and strength, and honour, and glory, and blessing" (verse 12).

Who is this Lamb? It is Jesus Christ, the Son of God. It is the One of whom John the Baptist said, "Behold the Lamb of God, that taketh away the sin of the world" (John 1:29). It is the One who died on the cross, who was for sinners slain. In heaven He still bears the marks of sacrifice. No wonder the multitudes sang, "Worthy is the Lamb who was slain."

The text says, "Worthy is the Lamb to receive." In this world we put the emphasis on our receiving. We are continually asking that we receive something. The Christian life begins with our receiving forgiveness and salvation. Every day we receive added blessings and one day we expect to receive everything in glory. But doesn't Christ yearn to receive something from us? Doesn't He yearn for our gratitude, our worship, our praise? The throng in heaven tells us that He is worthy to receive certain things.

I. He Is Worthy to Receive Power

The German nation considered that Hitler was worthy to receive power, so they gave it to him in abundance and he used it in the wrong way. But Christ always uses power in the right way. He used it to create the world. He uses it now to save and bless men. Someday He will use it to raise us up and give us a home in heaven.

In South Carolina a little boy sat in a country church during a revival service. The sermon was on "Heaven." The preacher said, "If you do not accept Christ, you will not go to heaven." The little boy was deeply moved. That night he went back to church and heard a sermon on "What Must I Do to Be Saved?" He went home and went to bed, but he could not sleep. When he came to the breakfast table the next morning his eyes were red from weeping. He said to his mother, "Mother, I feel awful sinful." She told him that there was only one way to get rid of his sins and that was to come to Jesus for forgiveness.

He went to the field to plow that morning and when he came to the end of the first row he felt that he could bear his burden no longer. He went over to a corner of the rail fence and began to pray. "Oh, God," he cried, "I am awful sinful. I want to be saved and go to your heaven. If I must accept Your Son as my Saviour I am telling You that I accept Him right now." The little boy was saved right there in that fence corner and that night he went forward in the church and confessed Christ as Saviour and Lord. God later called him to preach. He grew up to be Dr. Robert G. Lee, certainly one of the greatest preachers America has ever known. Oh, the power of Christ in a human life!

Christ promised that we would have power, also. He said, "Ye shall receive power, after that the Holy Ghost has come upon you" (Acts 1:8). If you are willing to throw sin out of your life and let Jesus take full charge, you can have a spiritual power to bless the world.

II. He Is Worthy to Receive Riches

He was not rich on earth; He had no place to lay His head. Paul said, "For ye know the grace of our Lord Jesus Christ, that, though he was rich, yet for your sakes he became poor, that ye through his poverty might be rich" (II Corinthians 8:9). He was so poor that he was dependent on the love gifts ministered by some good women. He preached from a borrowed boat, He was buried in a borrowed tomb. He owned only one thing here — the cross was His own. Ah, but He is rich in heaven. God has made Him an heir of all things. All things are His, heaven and glory belong to Him.

And Jesus wants to share those riches with us. When we come to Him, we become "joint heirs" with Him of all the good things of heaven. God has some poor people on this earth. They find it difficult to make both ends meet, and they seldom have enough to eat or wear. But one day Christ will take them to glory where they shall never lack for anything. They will share with Christ in all of His riches. Yes, once we were all poor lost sinners, we owned nothing up there. But now we have a mansion in the sky. All the riches of glory are waiting for us, because they are His and we are His.

III. He Is Worthy to Receive Wisdom

Wisdom is more than knowledge. Wisdom is the knowledge of how rightly to apply knowledge. Solomon prayed for knowledge and God gave it to him abundantly. But when Jesus came He said, "A greater than Solomon is here" (Matthew 12:42). Jesus was the wisest man who ever lived; He never made a mistake. There was nothing wrong in anything He ever said or thought or did. The chief priests and Pharisees one day sent officers to arrest Him, but they came back without Him. They said, "No man ever spoke like this man. We did not dare to arrest Him." They were astounded at His wisdom.

God has promised wisdom for us, also. "If any of you lack wisdom, let him ask of God, that giveth to all men liberally, and upbraideth not; and it shall be given him" (James 1:5). Every day we need wisdom. Every day we stand at the crossroads. Every day there are decisions to be made. Confronted with life's baffling questions, we ask, "What must I do?" And Jesus says, "Come with Me and I will show you the way." Listen to Psalm 37:5, "Commit thy way unto the LORD; trust also in him; and he shall bring it to pass." If we but follow Him, His wisdom shall be ours.

Christmas Evans was an effective Welsh preacher. He preached often, but felt the need of more wisdom. One day, on the way to an engagement, he stopped by the roadside, tied his horse to a tree and prayed for three hours. After that he was called a "God-intoxicated man." His congregations doubled. He preached for 53 years and hundreds were saved under his ministry. Christ shared His wisdom with him.

IV. HE IS WORTHY TO RECEIVE STRENGTH

There is a difference between strength and power. A man may be powerful, but have no moral strength. Samson was powerful, but he was not strong. Christ was strong. He faced every test and never flinched. Satan hurled all his force against Him, but He stood as firm as Gibraltar. He didn't give an inch. Satan could not get the least hold on Him.

You and I are weak. Satan is a million times stronger than we are. He comes at us and we falter and fall. But we are promised strength in the struggle. We are to cry to Jesus when we are tempted. Then all the resources of heaven will be rushed to our side. Yes, we are weak, but in Him we can overcome the evil one.

V. He Is Worthy to Receive Honor

We are great people to honor men. We honor the athlete, the actor, the politician, the scientist. Some of them are unworthy, but Christ is worthy of all the honor that men and angels give Him. What man has ever done for mankind what Christ has done? He found men sunk in sin, going down toward death and hell. But He lifted them up, made them to become sons of God and set their feet on the road to heaven.

Jesus will share His honor with us. He said, "If any man serve me, him will my Father honour" (John 12:26). If you follow Christ, all the honor and glory that are His in heaven will be shared with you.

Dr. Barnardo ran an orphanage in London. One day a ragged boy came to the door and asked for admission. Mr. Barnardo said, "But I don't know you. Who are you? Who will recommend you?" The boy held up his ragged coat and showed Mr. Barnardo his torn trousers. "Please sir," he said, "I thought these would be all I needed to recommend me." You know what the good man did? He caught up the boy in his arms, took him in and gave him a home.

Once we were deep-dyed sinners. We had nothing good to recommend us. Our own righteousness was as "filthy rags." But we came to Jesus in faith and He took us in His arms and claimed us as His very own. One day we poor sinners will share all the honor with Him in heaven.

VI. He Is Worthy to Receive Glory

On earth He had no glory. He turned His back upon it all when He left heaven. He was born in a stable and reared in a carpenter's poor home. He lived a lonely life; He was persecuted and mistreated. Finally He was crucified on a cruel cross. But now all the glory of heaven is His. God has highly exalted Him and given Him a name which is above every name. His glory is so great in heaven that no light is ever needed there. His glory fills the place with the most brilliant light.

A man tells about going to see the coronation of Edward VII of England. Princes were there and princesses and earls and dukes and others of high rank and nobility. The crowd looked on these nobles with respect, but when the king arrived all eyes left off looking at the others and every eye was fastened on the king. People and things of this world hold our attention now, but when we see Jesus He will be so glorious that we'll forget all else and gaze on His wondrous glory.

> All hail the power of Jesus' name!
> Let angels prostrate fall;
> Bring forth the royal diadem,
> And crown Him Lord of all.

Yes, He is worthy to receive glory and He invites us to share that glory with Him.

VII. He Is Worthy to Receive Blessing

It is said that Queen Victoria often visited the Old Folks' Homes of England. As she passed among them, they could add nothing to her glory or her possessions. But many of them said, "God bless your Majesty." You and I can add nothing to the glory of Christ, but we can say, "Bless the Lord, O my soul: and all that is within me, bless his holy name" (Psalm 103:1). And all through eternity, as we enjoy the things He has prepared for us, surely we shall continually be blessing His name.

As you think of what Jesus has done, is doing and will do for you, don't you want to give Him your very best in this life? And don't you long for the time when you can fall at His feet and thank Him for it all? Yes, but what are you doing now to show Him you appreciation? Are you trusting Him, are you serving Him, are you following Him? Are you active in His church? Are you helping to spread the Gospel? Oh, let's be faithful to Him, let's be busy for Him.

Dr. O. L. Powers was a pastor in North Carolina. He had a long siege of sickness and the doctors feared that he would die. But his deacons met often and prayed for him. Soon he was on the road to recovery. When he was able to leave the house he went down to the drug store and asked the druggist, "How much do I owe you?" The druggist replied, "You were sick a long time and your bill is a large one." Then he told the preacher the amount. The preacher said, "I can't pay you now, but I will as soon as I can." He started out the door with a heavy heart, but the druggist called him back. He said to the preacher, "But look at the last page." And on that page he saw the words, "Paid in full." "Yes," said the druggist, "a good friend of yours came in and paid it all." With gratitude in his heart the preacher left the store, but he said his soul was singing with another song. He said, "I was thinking of another debt, the debt of sin. But I was remembering that Jesus paid that debt in full and I was free."

Oh, my friends, Jesus paid the debt for us, freed us from the penalty of sin and set our feet on the pathway to glory. He is worthy to receive the best we have every day. Are you willing to give it to Him? Are you?

8
Though Your Sins Be as Scarlet
Isaiah 1:18

This is one of the greatest texts in the Bible. I am glad it is there. Now we know that any man, even though he has gone far away from God and deep down into sin, can have all of his sins taken away. The scarlet can be as snow. The crimson can be as wool.

We see in this text that God is a reasonable God. He is a gentleman. He never forces anything down our throats. He talks to us, He reasons with us, He counsels us, but He leaves it up to us as to whether we will follow Him or not. He is simply saying in this text, "I want to sit down and talk things over with you. Let's reason this thing out and I promise you that if you will put your trust in Me I'll wash all your sins away."

God knows this. If you are reasonable, if you are sensible, if you will listen to Him and use your intellect, you will do the right thing and be saved.

So let us draw this picture. God sits in one chair and a lost sinner sits in another. Filled with compassion and love, what will God say to the sinner?

I. GOD SAYS — "YOU MUST REALIZE THAT YOU ARE A SINNER"

Here is the way He puts it: "All have sinned and come short of the glory of God" (Romans 3:23). "All we like sheep have gone astray; we have turned every one to his own way" (Isaiah 53:6). "There is none righteous, no, not one" (Romans 3:10). "The heart is deceitful above all things, and desperately wicked" (Jeremiah 17:9).

Now God is not merely saying that we have done some sinful things. He is also saying that we have a sinful nature. Some people say, "I'll cut off this sin; I'll give up that bad habit." You can do that and still be a sinner. God is not as much concerned with the fact of your various sins as He is that you are a sinner.

An apple tree is not an apple tree because it bears apples. It bears apples because it is an apple tree. You are not a sinner because you sin. You sin because you are a sinner, you have a sinful nature. Angels don't sin because they are angels. But you do sin because you are a sinner.

You can get rid of some sins, even of many sins, and still be a sinner. In the early years of my ministry I preached in a revival in a country community. On the first day of the meeting a good woman said to me, "Some of the young men in our community are playing cards and gambling. I want you to preach a sermon against gambling." Now if I had succeeded in getting these young men to give up their gambling, that would not have solved the problem, so I didn't preach about gambling. I preached Christ who could save from all sin, and in the providence and grace of God these young men came and heard the message, were converted and gave up their gambling. Men are not changed by giving up a few sins. They are changed by conversion to Christ, then they have a power to overcome their sins.

I once had a young man in my Sunday school class who was not a Christian. Liquor was his besetting sin. I tried without success to win him to Christ. After he had been on a drunken spree for several days he was ill at his home. I visited him and he said, "Preacher, I am going to quit drinking. The doctor told me that if I continued to drink I might go out like a light one of these days." His resolution did not last long, because it was born of fear and not from the New Birth. What he needed to do was not merely to give up something. He needed a new life, he needed to be born again.

We notice that God says we have gone astray "like sheep." Not like dogs or horses — they can find their way home. But when a sheep goes astray someone must go after it and bring it back home. Do you see here how practical the Holy Spirit was in writing the Bible? So Jesus the great Shepherd came down to earth. He came looking for His sheep, that He might save them and bring them home.

God also says that we have turned to our "own ways." There are just two ways to turn, our way or God's way. If you have not turned to God's way you are going your own way and that's the way of sin, the way that leads to hell.

So God says, "You must realize that you are a sinner and that sinners are lost." Why does God want you to feel that way? Because if you see yourself as a sinner, you'll feel your need of a Saviour. It's when a man knows he is drowning that he feels the need of a rescuer. It's when a man knows he is sick that he feels the need of a doctor. It's when a man knows he is a sinner that he feels the need of a Saviour. Why don't you say to the God who reasons with you, "Yes, Lord, I know I am a sinner."

II. GOD SAYS, "I LOVE YOU IN SPITE OF YOUR SIN"

"But," you say, "how can that be possible? If I am a sinner, how can a holy and righteous God love me? I don't love the unlovely, I don't love those who oppose me. How can God love me when I have sinned so grievously against Him?" Well, that's why He is God. He can do what you can't do. He hates your sin, but He loves you.

Suppose that you had a child and a dread disease was eating that child's life away. You would not love the disease, but you would love the child. So God hates the sin that is ruining you, but He loves you.

How do we know that God loves a sinner? We go to Calvary and see God's only Son dying on a cross. We cry out, "Why does God allow this?" One answer comes back from the skies, "For God so loved the world that he gave his only begotten Son, that whosoever believeth in him should not perish, but have everlasting life." A father loves a prodigal son, a mother loves a wandering child, a wife loves an unfaithful husband, a patriot loves his country. But all of this is nothing compared to God's love for sinners.

How wide and deep is God's love? Well, think of such men as Hitler and Mussolini and all the evil that came out of their lives and plans. Of course God did not approve of what they did. But if these men had turned to Him in genuine repentance, He would have forgiven them. He loved them but not their deeds. Maybe you are saying, "I have stooped pretty low. I have done things I don't want anyone else to know about." That doesn't matter. The thing that does matter is that God loves you and every other sinner on earth.

Romans 5:8 tells us that, "God commendeth his love toward us, in that, while we were yet sinners, Christ died for us." This verse doesn't say that He extended His love and gave His Son for perfect people, but for sinners.

Now God's love calls for a response. What are you going to do about His love? Are you going to turn your back on it? Are you simply going to ignore it? Don't do that, my friend. Let that great love for you break your heart and bring you to Him.

III. GOD SAYS, "I DON'T WANT YOU TO PERISH"

In II Peter 3:9 we read that "God is not willing that any should perish, but that all should come to repentance." Ezekiel 33:11 says, "As I live, saith the Lord GOD, I have no pleasure in the death of the wicked; but that the wicked turn from his way and live."

We are told that Eichmann and the Nazi butchers killed six million Jews. They seemed to derive pleasure from thrusting these people into the gas chambers and watching them die. They were men, evil men. God is not like that. He gets no pleasure from seeing someone suffer. So all the way through the Bible He is pleading with men to turn away from sin and live.

In Noah's time the world was filled with rankest sinners. God did not want to see them die so He sent Noah to preach repentance and salvation to them. He didn't want the people of Nineveh to die, so He sent Jonah to preach to them. He doesn't want to see you die, so He sent His Son to die for you and provide a way of escape for you.

The railroads have their efficient red-light warning systems. When the engineer peers into the night and sees the red light shining, he knows there is danger ahead and brings his engine to a stop. To go through the red light might mean death to him and to his passengers. In like manner God has set up His red lights along life's pathway to save men from hell. What are some of them? There is the Bible, then there are the gospel sermons you have heard, there is the church, there is the witness of a friend, there are the sorrows of life, and, finally, there is the Holy Spirit. If you crash through all of these warning signals you will go down to hell. Yet, all the while God is saying, "I don't want this to happen to you. I've done everything necessary to save you."

IV. God Says, "I Offer You Salvation Through My Son"

The sinner deserves only to die. But God loves the sinner so much, in spite of his sin, that He sent His Son to die in the sinner's place. Do you remember Barabbas? He was in prison on the day that Christ was to be crucified. But Pilate, the governor, had a custom of releasing a prisoner on a certain holiday. He gave the people the privilege of choosing the one to be released. So he brought both Jesus and Barabbas out and placed one on his right side and one on his left. Then he asked the mob, "Which one shall I release unto you?" Think of the choice they had to make. On one side stood the sinless Son of God who had gone about doing good. On the other side was Barabbas, whose evil deeds were known to everyone. What choice did the people make? They cried out, "Release unto us Barabbas and crucify Christ."

So Barabbas went free and Jesus died. As He hung on the cross I can imagine that Barabbas crept close to the cross and said, "There's where I should have died today, but, thank God, that wonderful man died in my place." That should be the cry of every man. As you think of your sin, as you know you deserve death, as you see Jesus dying on that cross in your stead, you ought to cry out, "I belonged there, I had sinned, I deserved death. But He died there for me, so I'll take Him as my Saviour and love Him and serve Him all my life."

Some years ago a man was gloriously saved and someone asked him how it happened. He answered, "I swapped with Jesus. I swapped my sin for His salvation. I gave Him my sin and He gave me everlasting life." That's what happens in salvation and it's the most wonderful bargain a man can ever make.

Salvation is a simple matter but men try to make it difficult. A certain lawyer said, "Before I was saved I used to think that if I ever became a Christian it would have to be in some great center of learning where all of my questions could be answered. But instead I was saved in a rescue mission as I knelt at the front with human derelicts all around me. When I knelt I had all my questions, when I arose they were gone. God didn't answer them, He removed them." Oh, soul in sin, don't go around looking for arguments and answers, just come to Jesus. He is the answer.

Christ is your only hope. He saves you when you come to Him in simple faith. All your good works, all your gifts, all your kindness to others, all your form and ritualism can never save you. Only Jesus can do that.

I happened to be in Lima, Peru, on Corpus Christi Day. All the stores closed their doors. Thousands of people gathered in the square in front of the cathedral, while other thousands stood or sat inside. As I took my place in front of the cathedral I saw a long procession of priests and altar boys coming out. In a few minutes the bishop came out, seated on his throne. Several priests carried the throne and several others carried the canopy over the bishop. They walked around several blocks in the downtown area. They stopped at some type of shrine at every corner and celebrated mass. Hundreds of solemn-faced people followed the procession through the town, but there was no peace or happiness on their faces.

Men simply do not find peace and salvation in such religious ceremonies. The Bible says they must come to the Lord with a broken and a contrite heart. Then and then only can they find the peace that passes all understanding. When a man says, "My heart is burdened with my sin, but I now humbly repent of it all and simply trust Christ for my salvation," in that minute he is saved and all the bells of heaven begin to ring out for joy.

Here is a man who comes home at night, all tired out. He says to his wife, "What must I do to find rest?" She replies, "Believe on that chair and you will find rest." "I do believe," he says, "I have always believed in that chair, but I am still weary. What else must I do?" Then she says, "Trust the chair, commit yourself to it. Give yourself up to it. Lean on it with all your might." Then he sits down and it feels so good that he says, "I'm resting now. Why didn't you tell me to trust the chair and commit myself to it? The moment I sat down I began to rest." When you say to me that you want to be saved I say to you, "Believe on the Lord Jesus Christ and thou shalt be saved." Then you say, "Do you mean that I am just to believe in Him in my mind? I've always done that. I believe He was the Son of God and that He died on the cross." But I say to you, "Faith means more than that. Trust your all to Him, all the past, present and future. Commit everything to Him. Lean entirely on Him." And the minute you do that you will find rest and peace and eternal life. You will be able to say, "All is mine since I trusted Him."

Do I hear someone saying, "That's all very good, but I have plenty of time left yet in which to be saved." A man in the Bible said the same thing, but God said, "Thou fool, this night thy soul shall be required of thee" (Luke 12:20). And that night he died. How much more time do you have?

One of our missionaries in the Orient had a bomb fall on his house. Four children were playing in the living room when the terrible crash came. In a few seconds four frightened little girls came out of the wreck with not a scratch on them. The youngest one said, "God saved us and nobody was killed, but if the next bomb hits us and kills us it will be all right, for we will go to heaven and be with Jesus and there will be no wars and guns up there."

Do you have that assurance? If you died tonight, where would you go? God says, "Come now, and though your sins be as scarlet they shall be as white as snow."

9

The Question We Never Ask
Jeremiah 8:6

Jeremiah has been called "the weeping prophet." He was a preacher's son and God called him to be a prophet. He sent him up and down the land to preach repentance to the people and to warn them of the wrath to come. And as he thought of God's goodness to His people and of their sin and idolatry, he wept like a brokenhearted angel.

Jeremiah stood up for righteousness and the people hated him. Let a preacher take a stand today for the right and he, too, will be hated by some. But Jeremiah remained true in spite of all opposition, thus setting an example for us.

In the text Jeremiah tells us that he listened for the penitent cry of one man, but in all the land there was none. No one said, "I have sinned, I am guilty." No one asked the question, "What have I done?" A man is in a pitiful condition when he never sees that he has done anything wrong. Yet there are many today who never make that admission. But as Christians we know that we are not what we ought to be. As we measure our lives against the life and teachings of Jesus, we see the need to repent and confess our sins every day. Then there are lost sinners who live as if there were no God, no Calvary, no Saviour. They need to cry out, "What have I done?"

This is the question that many never ask, "What have I done?" But today let's sit in judgment upon ourselves. Let's ask ourselves this pertinent question.

I. What Have I Done With Jesus Christ?

When Governor Pilate appeared before the bloodthirsty mob in Jerusalem he asked the question, "What shall I do with Jesus who is called Christ?" This is a question which every man must answer.

What can you do with Jesus? You can accept Him or reject Him. You can receive Him into your heart or leave Him alone. You can live for Him or for the world. You are the only one who can answer this question for yourself. The issue is between you and God. And all of life in this world and the world to come depends upon your answer to this question. Your happiness and usefulness in this world and your eternal destiny are determined by what you do with Jesus.

It is not a question of what others say or do. It is not a question of hypocrites in the church. It is a question of what you, personally, have done with Jesus Christ. Have you met Him face to face in the matter of your sin? Have you experienced His saving grace? Have you formed a vital connection with Him? Have you been born again?

Listen to what God says about the matter: John 3:36 — "He that believeth on the Son hath everlasting life: and he that believeth not the Son shall not see life; but the wrath of God abideth on him." John 3:18 — "He that believeth in him is not condemned: but he that believeth not is condemned already, because he hath not believed in the name of the only begotten Son of God." Romans 10:9, 10 — "That if thou shalt confess with thy mouth the Lord Jesus, and shalt believe in thine heart that God hath raised him from the dead, thou shalt be saved. For with the heart man believeth unto righteousness; and with the mouth confession is made unto salvation."

If you are not a Christian I'll tell you what you have done with Jesus. You have trampled the Son of God underfoot. You have turned your back on your Best Friend.

You have said to a loving God, "I don't care for Your Son." You've missed the best of life. You are under God's condemnation. You are on the way to hell. Now what ought you to do? You should come to Jesus, just as you are. You should receive Him as your Saviour and live at your best for Him. Then He will fill your life with joy and take you to heaven.

Christian, what have you done with Jesus? You have allowed Him to save you, but is that all there is to your Christian life? What have you done as He has asked you for your time, your talent, your tithe? Have you said, "I am too busy"? Well, that is like the spring saying that it has no time for water. That is like the tree saying that it has no time for the sap. That is like the sun saying, "I have no time for light." That is like the garden saying, "I have no time for the flowers." Yet the Christian ought to give His best, His all, to Christ.

So I ask you the question, "What have you done and what are you doing with Jesus?" If your answer doesn't satisfy you, come to Him today and say, "Lord, from now on You can count on me. You can have my best."

II. What Have I Done With His Church?

The Lord Jesus knew that when we became new creatures in Christ we would need something onto which we could tie our lives. So He put the church down here. It is His will that we live in it and serve through it. By such means His Gospel is carried to the ends of the earth. It is, therefore, the privilege and the duty of every Christian to get into a New Testament church and to love, serve in and support that church.

But think of the hundreds of church members who never go to church, who never give a penny, who live as if there were no God, no Saviour, no church. Are they saved? We do not know. We are not their judge. But if

I were a Christian and paid so little attention to the church, I would feel that there was something terribly wrong with me.

The church of Jesus Christ blesses us in the most vital hours of life, in time of marriage, in times of sorrow, in time of death. The church is God's divine agency which has preserved the gospel message over the ages. If there were no churches, you and I would not know of the Saviour. If our churches were allowed to die the land would sink into despair and would be too much like hell for us to live in.

You can neglect the church now, but some day when you face God, He will say, "I put My church down there for your benefit. I wanted you to be in it, serving Me and mankind. Why weren't you faithful?

III. WHAT HAVE I DONE WITH THE HOLY SPIRIT?

God sent the Holy Spirit into the world for a double purpose. First, He was to convict sinners of their lost condition, second, He was to do a work in the hearts of Christians. Are you allowing Him to work in your heart? When you hear His still small voice, are you willing for Him to have His way in your life?

In Galatians 5:22, 23 the fruits of the Spirit are listed. These are the things that will come out of your life when you let the Spirit have His way with you. Let us look at this list.

1. *Love* — Do you love your fellow Christians, your neighbors, your enemies? When people treat you badly can you still love them? Have you grown enough in grace to say, like Jesus, "Father forgive them, they know not what they do"?

How is the world going to know that you are a Christian? Not by your gifts, your big talk, your loud prayers. But here it is, "By this shall all men know that you are my disciples, if ye have love one to another" (John 13:35). The Holy Spirit causes us to love others.

2. *Joy* — Are you a joyful Christian, or do people think of you as a crab? No one will really be impressed with your brand of religion if you wear a long face.

3. *Peace* — Do you have a peaceful heart or are you always worrying? God fed three million people in the desert without a bakery or a supermarket. Their shoes did not get old, their clothes didn't wear out. Don't you think He can take care of you? He says, "Seek ye first the kingdom of God and his righteousness, and all these things shall be added unto you" (Matthew 6:33). Do you have peace in your heart?

4. *Longsuffering* — Life becomes hard and difficult at times. Do you quit and give up in despair? Or do you hold on, knowing that "all things work together for good to them that love God"? (Romans 8:28).

5. *Gentleness* — Has the Holy Spirit made you a gentle person? Or do the store clerks and others feel that you are the snappy and demanding type?

6. *Goodness* — This means just plain old-fashioned goodness. The Holy Spirit within creates that goodness.

7. *Meekness* — Are you meek or do you think too highly of yourself? If we could buy some people for what they are worth and sell them for what they think they are worth, we could become millionaires.

8. *Faith* — How much faith do you have in God? He made the world. He keeps it going. When the least ill wind blows, do you go all to pieces? If you worry you don't trust. If you trust you don't worry.

9. *Self-Control* — Do you fly off the handle and lose your temper at the least provocation? A man can control a train, a ship, a plane, but it takes the help of the Holy Spirit to control tongue and temper.

Yes, what have you done with the Holy Spirit? He

wants to come into your life and make it sweet and fine and useful. Will you let Him have His way with you? Or will you say, "I'm going my way"?

IV. What Have I Done With the Bible?

Today we have great Sunday schools, Bible classes and Bible conferences. On the other hand the land is filled with an abysmal ignorance of God's Word. Some time ago I asked a congregation in a very strong church how many of them had read the book of Hezekiah. Scores of hands went up. I asked where one could find the expression, "every tub must sit on its own bottom." Some said it could be found in the Old Testament, some in the New!

A boy writes an ardent love letter to his sweetheart. When she receives it, does she say, "The next time I have a holiday I'll read that letter"? No, she tears it open and reads it over and over until she knows it by heart. Yet Christians say, "I have a love letter from the Lord. It is called the Holy Bible. Someday I'll take it down from the shelf and read it."

What are you doing with the Bible? It's dangerous for you to read it for it will cause you to make some changes in your life. It will make you give up some of your bad habits. It will make you want to be more faithful to your church. It will make you want to tithe. It will make you want to live less for the world and more for God. Yet every change will be for the better. Life will be much happier and more useful.

V. What Have I Done About Prayer?

We think of prayer as a one-way path to God. When we want something we go and ask God for it in the name of Christ. We thank God for that privilege. In John 15:7 we read, "If ye abide in me, and my words abide in you, ye shall ask what ye will, and it shall be done unto you."

Now notice the condition in this verse. If we are living for Jesus, if we are abiding in Him and obeying His commands, we have a right to ask Him for what we need. Too many people feel that they can go along through life, forgetting about God, then when they get in a hole He will rush to their side. But God's promises are not to the sinful, the neglectful, the indifferent. He promises His best only to those who are abiding in Him.

But prayer has a reflex action. Prayer does more for the one who prays than merely getting things from God. Often we go to God and ask Him for something and He says "No." But somehow God changes us and causes us to know that it was for our own good that He did not give us what we prayed for. Then we find contentment in doing without that thing.

A young man left home and went to the great city. Months went by and his mother did not hear a word from him. Finally she could stand it no longer so she went to the city and found the boy. The first thing he said to her was, "Mother, your face has changed." And she answered, "Son, your mother has been praying a lot since you left." Prayer changes things and prayer changes people.

VI. WHAT HAVE I DONE WITH MY POCKETBOOK?

What should we do about our money? The Bible answers that question in language easily understood. It tells us to bring our tithes and offerings to His storehouse, to be used for the cause of Christ around the world. As the Temple was the storehouse in ancient days, the New Testament church is the storehouse today. Many Christians believe in tithing but they don't have faith enough and consecration enough to practice it.

There ought to be two sides to your pocketbook. On one side there should be God's part, which is at least one-tenth. On the other side there is the other nine-tenths, which God graciously allows you to use for your own needs.

When a certain little boy started to Sunday school, his mother gave him two nickels. She told him that one nickel was for God and one for himself. As the boy walked down the street he dropped one of the nickels and it rolled away into the sewer. The boy said, "Good-by, God's nickel." God has to take the loss in many instances.

But the tither quickly learns that his nine-tenths goes much farther when he faithfully gives God His part. If I could influence you to tithe, God would bless you in such a manner that you would forever be grateful to me.

VII. What Have I Done As a Soul-Winner?

Jesus said, "Follow me and I will make you fishers of men" (Matthew 4:19). There are lost people all around us. Some of them are in our homes, some in our places of business, some in our social circle. Are we interested in them? Do they know that we care? Do we realize that lost condition before God? Have we told them that we are praying for them and that we are anxious to see them saved?

But we won't be very successful in winning others if our own lives are not what they ought to be. I held a meeting in a certain place and one night several people were saved, one of them a junior boy. After the service a well-dressed man about thirty-five years of age came up to me and said, "I have a little boy and I hope to see him take that step someday." Then I caught the odor of liquor upon his breath and I said, "If you expect that to happen, you had better live rightly before him. He looks to you as his example, you know." The man turned away, but I'm sure he got the message. The blind can't lead the blind.

A preacher in England applied for a position as an army chaplain. In order to test him the Chaplain General took out his watch and said, "All right, just imagine that I am a soldier dying on the battlefield. I have only three minutes to live. Can you tell me how to be saved?" The preacher floundered around for two minutes and the Chaplain General said, "I just have one minute left. What have you to say to me?" And all the preacher could do was to pull out his prayer book. The Chaplain General said, "No, that won't help in an hour like that."

Men are going down all around us. Do you have a message for them? Can you tell them how to be saved? Has your experience with Christ been genuine enough to pass it on to someone else? Christ crucified is the only remedy for sin, the only hope for sinners. Have you ever told anybody about Him?

VIII. WHAT HAVE I DONE WITH GOD'S WARNINGS?

God warns the unsaved. You are lost, you have no permanent lease on life, you may go out to face God at any minute. The Bible warns, "Boast not thyself of tomorrow, for thou knowest not what a day may bring forth" (Proverbs 27:1). Amos warns, "Prepare to meet thy God" (Amos 4:12).

God warns the backslider. You have been neglecting your simple Christian duties, you have been living for self only. God loves you; He warns you. Don't wait for His chastisement to bring you back to Him. I have often prayed by the bedside of backsliders who were sick. The tears would come into their eyes and they would say, "When I get well, I'll come back to church." But so many of them forgot their promises and later went back to their neglectful lives.

When I was a boy the news of the sinking of the Titanic stirred my soul. They said that this floating palace was unsinkable. When she left England bound for America on her maiden voyage, flags were flying, bands were playing,

The Question We Never Ask

everybody was happy. On Sunday night, as the ship plowed through the Middle Atlantic, the passengers were dancing and drinking. Then a message was relayed to the captain, "Look out for icebergs." But the captain smiled. The Titanic was unsinkable. A few minutes later a cry came from the crow's nest, "Iceberg ahead." The ship's engines were reversed but it was too late. There was a terrific crash and a gaping hole was torn in the hull of the ship. Before long the unsinkable Titanic went to the bottom of the Atlantic. Over 1,600 people went to their death.

This disaster occurred because the warnings were not heeded. But there is something more important. God is warning us every day. He is telling us that life is short, that a day is coming when we must give an account to Him. We are wise only when we heed His warnings.

On the first of the year merchants take an inventory. They want to learn what stock they have on hand and what they need. It would be good for you to do the same thing. Look at your life. Are you satisfied with it? Are you giving your best to God? Are you obedient to His voice? Are you living a good, faithful life? Check up on yourself. Ask God to forgive your sins and shortcomings. Then turn about and ask Him to help you to be better and live better.

Lee Lockett graduated from Baylor University. He married a fine Christian girl and they went as missionaries to darkest Africa. The years went by and God gave them three wonderful children. In time the children were sent back to America to escape an epidemic of African fever. They stayed with their grandparents near Abilene, Texas. One day as they were driving down a country road, the children were trapped in a flash flood rushing down a creek bed and all three of them were drowned. The brokenhearted father and mother came back to America. Mr. Lockett's health failed and he died shortly afterward.

What did Mrs. Lockett do? Her children were gone and her husband was buried by their side. Now you would think that she would have settled down at home and lived a quiet life. But instead she said, "Let me go back and give the rest of my life to Africa and to Jesus."

That is real consecration. So I close by asking you the question of my text, "What have I done? What have I done with my life?" Oh, won't you come and give it to Jesus, who gave His all for you? You will never regret it.

10

The Doctrine of the New Birth
John 3:7

In God's dealings with man, there is always a divine side and a human side. We see that in the giving of the Bible. God inspired men and they wrote down what God had given them. It took God and man, working together, to produce the Bible. There is a human side and there is a divine side to Jesus Christ. He was born of a woman, that is the human side. But God through the Holy Spirit produced the virgin birth. That is the divine side.

There is a human side and there is a divine side to salvation. We call the human side "conversion" and this comes about through repentance and faith. We call the divine side "regeneration" and God brings this about. "As many as received him," that is the human side. "To them gave he power to become the sons of God," that is the divine side.

We learn the truth of regeneration when we hear Jesus talking to Nicodemus. Nicodemus was a good, clean, moral man, a ruler of the Jews. But he was not happy, he was not satisfied, there was no peace in his heart. He had heard of Jesus and he must have said, "If He ever comes my way I will pour out my heart to Him." Well, one day Jesus did come that way and Nicodemus slipped out under the cover of darkness to talk to Him.

He began the conversation by complimenting Jesus, but Jesus brushed the compliment aside. He probed deep into Nicodemus' heart and said, "Ye must be born again." Then Nicodemus asked, "How can I enter again into my mother's womb and be born again?" Jesus said, "What I mean is that you have been born of the flesh, but now you need to have a spiritual birth. The wind blows and you hear it, but you don't know where it came from nor where it is going. So is everyone that is born of the spirit. It is a mysterious change which comes from God."

Jesus further explained by saying, "As Moses lifted up the serpent in the wilderness, even so must the Son of man be lifted up: That whosoever believeth in him should not perish, but have eternal life" (John 3:14, 15). Then Jesus spoke the greatest words that ever fell upon the ears of mankind, "For God so loved the world, that he gave his only begotten Son, that whosoever believeth on him should not perish, but have everlasting life." We do not know what Nicodemus said in reply, but later events seem to prove that he was truly born again.

The truth of the New Birth is grossly neglected in many modern pulpits. Recently a university student said to me, "I am glad to hear some Bible preaching again. I don't hear it in the college church near our campus." I asked him what he did hear and he said, "I hear many sociological and psychological things, but nothing about man's lost condition, the death of Christ and the need of salvation."

It is said that George Whitefield preached 3,000 times on this text. Somebody asked him, "Why do you preach so often on being born again?" And he replied, "Because you must be born again."

I. THE MEANING OF REGENERATION

Literally it means a new birth. The regenerated person is one who has been reborn, born from above, born of God.

1. *Regeneration is a definite experience.* It is just as

definite as a physical birth. You can say, "That man was born in New York and in Florida." You mean that he was born physically in New York, but born spiritually in Florida. Someone asked Dwight L. Moody for a brief statement of his life. He wrote, "My name is Dwight L. Moody. I was born of the flesh in 1837, I was born of the spirit in 1856. I don't know when the flesh will die, but the spirit will never die."

One man can say, "I was born of the spirit of God on November 18, 1947, at a Sunday night service in the First Baptist Church." Another man may not be able to point to the very place and the exact moment. But both men can be sure they have been saved. They feel the witness of the spirit in their hearts and lives.

2. *Regeneration is an instantaneous experience.* It takes place in a moment's time. You may have a long experience leading up to it, but regeneration itself is instantaneous. I first met the word "instantaneous" as a teenage boy when I moved to the city. I boarded in a home where they had an instantaneous gas heater over the bathtub. You would strike a match and light the gas, and by the time you went around and turned on the water, it was hot. Now regeneration is like that. I don't understand it, but it is wonderful because it is of God. The Bible tells us that the minute a person comes to Christ the Holy Spirit enters his heart. He is born again. "He that believeth on the Son has everlasting life."

Some years ago, in the early days of my ministry, I held a revival in the church where I was pastor. The meeting began on Sunday morning, but I did not give an invitation until Wednesday night. At that time fifteen people came forward confessing Christ, many of whom I had dealt with privately. The next day a woman of another faith came to me and rebuked me sharply. She said, "When I was saved I had to go to the mourner's bench and weep and pray for a week." But God never says this is necessary. Regeneration is instantaneous. It may take a week for you to make up your mind to receive Christ, but it doesn't take a week for Jesus to save you.

3. *Regeneration is a spiritual experience.* It is an inward thing, not outward. It is different from reformation. In reformation a man decides to drop his bad habits and adopt good ones. In regeneration he receives a new nature from God, which causes him automatically to give up his old sinful life.

There are certain birds in South America that have yellow feathers. But some naturalists made an experiment with these birds. They pulled out a few feathers and inserted a secretion from a frog in the wounds. When the feathers grew out again they were not yellow, but of a different color. The outward appearance of the birds had changed, but they were still the same birds. In like manner a man may change on the outside and that's reformation. A spiritual experience changes the inner man and that's regeneration. Reformation does not bring regeneration, but regeneration certainly brings reformation. The regenerated man is a "new man in Christ Jesus."

God the Holy Spirit is the agent in regeneration. He does it all. Jesus plainly told Nicodemus that the New Birth was wrought by the Holy Spirit. The instrument the spirit uses is the Word of God. He applies Bible truth to our hearts. He causes us to see by the Bible that we are lost. He causes us to see by the Bible that hell is our destiny. He causes us to see by the Bible that a Saviour died for us on the cross. He causes us to see by the Bible that we need to repent of our sin and trust Christ. And when we do this the Holy Spirit regenerates us. He makes us children of God.

A crowd of people gathered on a street corner and listened to a man as he extolled the blessings of socialism.

The man cried out, "Socialism can put a new coat on a man." A young man who had just been converted answered: "But Jesus Christ can put a new man in that coat." There it is. A spiritual experience makes a new man out of the old man. Only God can do that.

4. *Regeneration is a lasting experience.* It lasts forever and ever. You were born of a human father. That means that you are always his child, no matter what happens. And if you are born of God you are God's child forevermore. You may backslide, you may become wayward, but you are always His child. If you are born again, you can't be unborn.

Think how the ugly caterpillar becomes a lovely butterfly. First he is an ugly worm, crawling in the dust. Then one day that worm wraps himself in a cocoon. Later, on a warm day, that cocoon bursts open and a beautiful butterfly comes out. No longer is he a crawling worm, he is a multi-colored butterfly. He soars up toward the heavens and rests in the heart of the flowers. He may become wounded, he may fall to the ground, but there is no power on earth to make him a worm again.

So a man in his unregenerate state is a worm of the dust. Then the spirit of God lays hold upon him and works a wondrous change in his soul. He becomes a child of God. He soars up to sit in heavenly places in Christ Jesus. He may slip and fall, as so many do, but no power on earth can change him back to what he was. Yes, thank God, regeneration is an experience that lasts forever.

II. THE NECESSITY OF REGENERATION

One word simply jumps out of the text. It is the word, "must." There is no other way to get to heaven except through the new birth. We are not saved by our works, our zeal, our gifts, our good lives. We must be born again to be saved.

1. *We must be born again because of human depravity.* We have all sinned, we are the children of wrath, the sons of Satan. If we are ever to become children of God, we must be born into His family. God by nature is sinless, man by nature is a sinner. How can a sinful man ever go up to live with a sinless God? Something must happen to him. He must be born again.

We were born in sin and we have been sinning ever since. Some are big sinners, some are little sinners. Some are depraved sinners, some are moral sinners. Some are blatant and outspoken sinners, some are quiet and inoffensive sinners. But all are sinners and none can enter the kingdom of God unless he has been born again.

Recently I spoke to a man in the hospital about his personal salvation and he said, "I have always tried to live a decent life." And the majority of lost people think that salvation comes through decency and good works. They leave Christ and regeneration out, but Jesus said, "Ye must be born again."

Some people think if they are not great sinners, they have a better chance of getting to heaven than a wicked person. But this is not so. Let me illustrate. You and I go to a ball game, where the admission price is six dollars. You have two dollars and I have only one dollar. Which one of us stands the better chance of gaining admission? You know the answer. Neither one of us can get in. This is also true about getting into the kingdom of God. The moral man may have many more good works in his favor than the wicked man, but since the price of admission is the New Birth, he cannot get any closer to heaven than the worst man on earth.

Ah, but suppose we both wanted to get into the ball game and a rich man came along and gave us six dollars apiece. Then both of us could get in. Well, that's what Jesus did. The good man couldn't get into heaven on his

The Doctrine of the New Birth 103

own and neither could the wicked man. But Jesus saw their plight. He paid the price for them both. Now they can both get in. When they accept what Christ has done for them the spirit comes in, they are born again, they are on the way to heaven.

Let me refer to George Whitefield again. As a young man he went deep down into sin. Then one day he saw all the blackness of his heart but he didn't know what to do to be saved. First, he tried self-denial. He denied himself every luxury. He wore ragged clothes, he ate the coarsest food, he fasted twice a week, he gave money to the poor, he spent nights in prayer. But it was all in vain, he found no peace. Then he met John Wesley, who gave him a book entitled, *The Life of God in the Soul*. He read the book and became convinced that he must become a new creature in Christ Jesus. He laid hold upon the Lord by faith and the spirit came in and the change was wrought. He later preached to the Indians of America, the colored people of the West Indies, the miners of Scotland and in the select drawing rooms of London. And always his message was, "Ye Must Be Born Again."

Let me use another illustration. Suppose we had a law that no one could meet the president of the United States unless he had been born in our country. Now a Chinese gentleman comes and wants to meet the president. They tell him that the law says no one can meet the president who was not born in the United States. "But," says the man, "in China I am a man of influence and good standing." "That doesn't matter," he is told, "the law says you cannot meet the president if you were not born in America." Then he goes off and changes his name to John Smith and comes back with the same request. Again he receives the answer, "Except a man is born in the United States he cannot meet the president." He goes away again. He changes his clothes. He puts away the flowing robes of the Orient and dons a Hart Schaffner and Marx suit. Then he returns in American clothes, but again he receives the same answer, "The clothes make no difference, except a man be born in the United States he cannot meet the president."

We have no such law as this, but God does. And He has a right to make that law. He says, "Except a man be born again, he cannot enter my Kingdom." That man may change his name, he may speak the language of Zion, he may don the robes of morality. But all this will be of no avail. He must be born again. Someone has well said, "It is an everlasting calamity to be born and not to be born again."

III. The Mystery of the New Birth

Nicodemus was puzzled at Christ's words. "How can these things be?" he asked. And men today ask, "How can the Spirit enter my life and transform it?" Well, there are some mysteries we can never understand in this life. We don't understand the mystery of the physical birth, yet we don't doubt the reality of it. Why should we doubt the reality of the spiritual birth?

Now Jesus acknowledged that there was a mystery in the New Birth. He spoke of the wind and of how we can feel it and see the results of it, yet we know not where it is going. It is the same way with the New Birth. We feel it in our hearts, we see the results of it, but we don't understand its mystery.

Christ one day opened the eyes of a blind man. The Pharisees found the man and asked him how it happened. "I don't know," replied the man, "I can't explain it. But this one thing I know, I once was blind, but now I see." If you have been saved you, too, can say, "I don't understand all that happened but I do know this. When I turned to Jesus it happened. He came into my soul and made a new creature out of me. "

A preacher wanted to know more about the New Birth, so he went down to see an old sailor. "Do you know anything about the wind?" he asked the sailor. "I can't explain the wind," the sailor replied, "but I know when the wind blows I can hoist my sail and the wind will carry my boat across the water." You and I don't understand all about the New Birth, but when Christ speaks to the soul, we can respond as the sailor did in hoisting the sail and the winds of the spirit will sweep over our souls and start us on the journey to heaven.

I do not understand the secret of television. I do not know how a picture and a voice can come into my living room through a small black wire, but I am not going to throw my television out of the window. I don't understand how a black seed buried in the ground can produce a beautiful rose or lily or carnation, but I still love flowers.

And I don't understand how God's spirit can transform my whole life, but I thank God that He does just that when I surrender to Him. I am willing to leave the mystery to Him.

IV. The Power of Regeneration

Human experience bears testimony to the transforming power of God's spirit in human life. Many have felt that power and have witnessed it in the lives of others.

A group of atheists was criticizing the Bible. One of them spoke of creation, saying, "What man with any common sense could believe that several thousand years ago God stooped down, picked up a piece of mud, breathed on it, and changed it into a man?" A Christian man answered him by saying, "I cannot answer all the questions about creation, but this one thing I know. One night God stooped down and picked up the dirtiest piece of mud in this city, breathed upon it by His spirit and changed a gambling, drinking, thieving wretch into a man of God. I was that man. For 23 years I have not gambled, drunk or stolen. It is easy to raise a cheap sneer against the Bible, but you can't explain the change in my life outside of God." Yes, a changed life is the greatest proof of the power of the New Birth.

Often I have ridden by the home in Cartersville, Georgia, where Sam Jones lived. He was a dynamic Methodist evangelist. As a young man he was wild and reckless, a sinful drunkard. But as his father lay on his deathbed Sam fell down by the bedside and yielded his heart to Christ. God called him to preach and he went all over America, preaching the Gospel, and turning thousands to Christ. One day he preached in his home town and after the service a godless man came up to him and said, "Are you the same Sam Jones who used to drink and curse around Cartersville?" Mr. Jones assured him that he was the same man but changed by the power of God. "Well," said the man, "I know now that God has power to save wicked sinners. I'll yield to Him now, praying that He will save me as He did you."

My friend, you can be born again, too. God is waiting for you now. His arms are wide open to receive you. He is ready to regenerate you, to take you into His family, to carry you to heaven. What must you do? Just repent of your sins, turn your back on them and come by faith to Jesus Christ. God promises to save you in that moment.

In 1933 a man by the name of Harry Spencer was arrested for murder in Chicago. When he came to trial they said he was the vilest, most profane man ever to enter a courtroom. The newspapers called him "a man without a soul." He was tried and sentenced to die. But a good Christian woman became interested in him and went to the jail to see him. A deputy took her to his cell and said to

The Doctrine of the New Birth

Spencer, "Here is a lady to see you. Don't abuse her, be nice to her." He promised that he would be nice. The lady came and sat on a chair just outside of his cell. She looked with pity at the man, haunted, defeated, condemned to die.

She said, "I came because I am the mother of three boys. I love them with all my heart. I feel that you have been denied a mother's love, since she died quite young. Is your heart hungry for something?" He replied through his tears, "Yes, ma'am, it is." "You missed a mother's love," she said, "but I have come to tell you of a greater love." Then she told him the story of the prodigal son and of the penitent thief on the cross. "They tell me you are a fearless man, that you are not afraid of anything. I am going to ask you to do a hard thing. I am going to ask you to give your heart to Christ and to invite Him to come in and cleanse you from all sin. Will you do it? Spencer said, "I will," and the lady said, "Let us have a prayer."

After a fervent prayer, he said, "While you were praying I kept on saying to God, 'Oh, God, help a sinful crook like me as you did the thief on the cross.' Now I feel 40 pounds lighter." She left a Bible with the man and marked several passages for him to read. When she returned the next day he said, "Good morning, I am just twenty-four hours old. I read the third chapter of John about being born again. I was born again twenty-four hours ago. I have learned John 3:16. Let me say it to you."

He began to study the Bible and the nearer he came to the time of death, the happier he came to be. One day the Christian woman asked him, "Do you really mean it when you say you want to leave this world?" "Yes," he answered, "life means nothing to me now. I just want to go and see the Man who died for me." The last night of his life, a group of Christian friends came and held a service outside of his cell. That night he slept like a baby. When the lady went back to see him she said, "You seem mighty happy." He answered, "Yes, because I am so near to God." At 9 o'clock he thanked the lady for what she had done for him, then went to his death with a smile on his face and a song on his lips.

You are not the sinner that Harry Spencer was, but if you are without Christ, you need the New Birth as much as he did. And, thank God, you can have it. Turn your back on your sin, then come to Christ in simple faith. In the twinkling of an eye, you will be born again and on the way to an eternal home in heaven.

11

Jesus, Highest Over All
Matthew 26:36-46

The Taj-Mahal in India is said to be the most beautiful building in the world. Erected 300 years ago, it has been called, "The Gem of Buildings." An emperor built it in memory of his wife, whom he loved deeply. It took 20,000 men working 22 years to build it. It is annually visited by thousands of people. A certain gospel preacher visited the Taj-Mahal one day and looked upon the various idols around him. Then he went to the central part of the building and cried out: "Jesus, highest over all." Yes, Jesus stands above all the gods of all time. He is the highest figure of all the ages.

Mount Mitchell in North Carolina is 6,711 feet high, making it the highest point in America east of the Rockies. If you stood on some nearby mountain peak you would be obliged to look up to Mount Mitchell. Yet Mt. Whitney in California is 14,501 feet high, more than twice as high as Mt. Mitchell. But Mt. Everest in Asia is 29,000 feet high, twice as high as Mt. Whitney. If these three mountains were placed side by side, a man standing on the top of Mt. Mitchell would have to look up to Mt. Whitney and a man standing on Mt. Whitney would have to look up to Mt. Everest.

It is the same way with men. Here and there we find a great man, but there are others who tower above them. However if you stand with the tallest of men, the best of men, the greatest of men, you must always look up to

Jesus Christ. He is always highest above all others. He stands out as the ocean stands out above a drop of water, as the sun in its glory stands out above a ten-cent candle.

In the Garden of Gethsemane we read that "He went a little farther." He went a little farther physically there, but truly He has gone farther in many respects than any man who ever lived. Let us look at some ways in which Jesus has gone farther.

I. He Went Farther in His Nature Than Any Other Man

He was not only human, but divine. He was all of God, yet all of man. He was all of God that He might help us. He was all of man that He might sympathize with us. If you say that He was only a man, you cannot explain His life, His death, His influence over these twenty centuries.

Call the roll of all the great men. The list is a long one. But none of them can compare with Jesus. They had their flaws, their sins, their shortcomings. But Jesus had none. They had their weaknesses, but Jesus had none. A woman told me that she had been married to a man four years before she learned that he had a single fault! But over all the years no one has found any fault in Jesus.

You look around and say, "I am going to find the ideal man." You pick out a man with the finest qualities and say, "I have found him." Then one day you watch him lose his temper and you say, "He is as weak as I am, I must look higher." But you must look all the way to Jesus to find the ideal man. He is the only perfect Man who ever lived. Pilate said, "I find no fault in this just man." Sidney Lanier called him, "The Crystal Christ."

Follow the course of a river. In the valley you see a muddy stream. Then you go up high into the mountains to the source of the river and you find water that is pure and clear. As you study men you see that they are like muddy streams. Sin is always present. But go higher and higher and you come to Jesus. You will find His life clear as sunlight. There is no pollution, no sin there. Yes, Jesus went farther in His nature than any other man.

II. HE WENT FARTHER IN HIS POWER THAN ANY OTHER MAN

You can't study His life without being impressed by His power.

1. *He had power over nature.* On board ship one night He fell asleep. Soon a storm arose and the disciples waked Him, saying, "Carest thou not that we perish?" (Mark 4:38). He arose and spoke to the raging storm, "Peace be still." Suddenly the waves were as quiet as a babe asleep on its mother's breast. And His friends marveled, saying, "What manner of man is this, that even the winds and the sea obey him?" (Mark 4:41)

When the hungry crowds followed Him, He took two loaves and five fishes, blessed them and multiplied them, so that more than five thousand ate and were filled. On another night He came toward the ship, walking on the water, showing again His power over nature.

But why couldn't He demonstrate His power over nature? He made it, He made the land and the sea.

"All things were made by him: and without him was not any thing made that was made" (John 1:3). All things are subject unto Him, for He is the maker of all things.

2. *He had power over disease and death.* A certain woman had been sick for twelve years. Many doctors had ministered to her, and none could help her. But when she simply touched the hem of His garment, healing power flowed out to her from Him.

When He came down from the Mount of Transfiguration, a certain man ran to Him and kneeled before Him, crying out, "My son is lunatick, have mercy on him" (Matthew 17:15). And Jesus rebuked the devil that possessed the boy, and cast him out.

Jesus was going into Nain one day, when He met a funeral procession. A poor widow had lost her son, her sole support. Jesus, being moved with compassion, touched the young man back to life and restored him to the arms of his mother. He also brought Lazarus and the daughter of Jairus back from death unto life.

3. *He had power over men.* He must have had a dynamic personality, for men from all walks of life were attracted to Him. He could go to a tax-collector's office and say to Matthew, "Follow me." And Matthew left his tax books to become the writer of another book, the first book in the New Testament. He could take a simple profane fisherman like Simon and turn him into Peter, the great preacher of Pentecost. He could take a murderous Pharisee like Saul and change him into Paul, the mighty apostle to the Gentiles.

And He still has this same power to change men. He is still making men over and giving them new life.

III. HE WENT FARTHER IN HELPFUL SERVICE THAN ANY OTHER MAN

The biographies of some men could read, "He went about making money," or "he went about having a good time," or "he went about seeking to elevate self," or "he went about indulging himself." But here in five words is the biography of the Lord Jesus, "he went about doing good" (Acts 10:38).

With all of His power, He used none for Himself. Always it was used for others. When He saw anyone who was sick or in trouble or in sorrow, His heart went out to them and He reached out a helping hand.

In the early colonial days a preacher by the name of John Weatherford preached the Gospel in Virginia. He spoke out boldly for Christ. The high authorities hounded him and sought to silence him. He won scores of people to Christ, but had to baptize them by night to avoid being seen by the authorities. Finally they put him in prison. Yet they could not stop him from preaching. The crowds filled the jailyard and he would reach his hands through the bars and preach to them. Wicked men came and slashed his hands almost into ribbons. A man who wrote the story of this preacher said, "I went to his funeral and when I saw the white scars on his hands, I knew they were the marks of the Lord Jesus."

That's real service to God and humanity. But that's nothing compared to the service Jesus rendered to broken humanity.

IV. HE WENT FARTHER IN THE CONQUEST OF TEMPTATION THAN ANY OTHER MAN

Here He is as a young man with all the human desires and feelings of any normal young man. The devil came against Him with three fierce temptations, but each time He defeated Satan and beat him back. But let us not think that these were all the temptations He had. We are told that Satan "departed from him for a season" (Luke 4:13). Surely this implies that He was often tempted, but always He conquered the tempter. Temptations come to people of all ages, but the fiercest ones come to young people. That's when you need the help of the Saviour. When temptations come you need to stay close to Him and call on Him for help.

In ancient times a citadel in France was besieged by its enemies. The day came when the enemy felt sure they could march in and take over. But they found the citadel empty. The French had found an underground passage and had escaped during the night. And when temptations beset us, when the devil assails us at our weakest points, we have a way of escape through Christ.

V. He Went Farther in Submission to God's Will Than Any Other Man

With His life before Him, He let God map out the plans for that life. He knew that God's way for Him would lead to a cross, but He did not falter. When He came to the end of the way that cross was waiting for Him and He willingly died upon it.

We read that He "set his face to go to Jerusalem" (Luke 9:51). He knew the suffering that awaited Him there, but He did not turn, He did not flinch. The cross was His goal and nothing could turn Him aside from it. Why did He do it? Because He knew this was the Father's will and He joyfully submitted to that will. He could say, "I do always those things which please my Heavenly Father." Oh, that we could say that!

During World War I the steamship *Lusitania* was on a voyage carrying hundreds of passengers. A German submarine lurked in the depths, bent on death and destruction. Soon a torpedo was loosed toward the *Lusitania*. The mistress of the sea, mortally wounded, trembled, floundered and went down. It was a horrible hour. The passengers rushed to the lifeboats. Everyone wanted to live.

A man named S. T. Moodie was on the deck, ready to embark to safety in a lifeboat. But he saw a woman without a lifebelt, a poor woman from the steerage section of the ship. He quickly took off his lifebelt and gave it to the woman. She was saved, but Moodie went down to a watery grave. That was fine, splendid. But Jesus did more than that to save sinful, sinking humanity. This was the Father's will for Him.

VI. He Went Farther in Absolute Giving of Himself

You and I live and work to gain happiness and profit and pleasure for ourselves. We seldom give ourselves away for others. But Jesus did just that. He took His life and gave it away. He said, "I have power to lay down my life and I have power to take it up again" (see John 10:18). And, using that power, He laid down His life for us.

If He suffered only physical death that would have been enough. But there was more. There was an inner, deeper, spiritual suffering which we can never fully understand. On the cross He cried, "My God, my God, why hast thou forsaken me?" He was bearing our sin in His body and that sin had separated even the Son from God. He suffered more in spirit than in body. And in it all He was giving Himself more than any other man.

VII. He Has Gone Farther in Influence on the World Than Any Other Man

He said, "Except a corn of wheat fall into the ground and die, it abideth alone: but if it die, it bringeth forth much fruit" (John 12:24). He became that grain and gave Himself and has been bearing fruit over the centuries.

Herod killed scores of babies and nothing was said about it. But when the Lindbergh baby was kidnaped the world was upset. This shows the influence of Jesus upon human thought. Women were once little more than slaves, but now they occupy an exalted position, thanks to the influence of Jesus. The hospitals all over the world, the childrens' homes, the care of the aged, all these things attest to the influence of Jesus Christ. For over 1,900 years He has gone up and down the world, touching lives and making them sweeter, better, richer, fuller.

John the Baptist came preaching repentance and baptizing converts, but he was dominated by Jesus. Paul was easily one of the world's greatest men, but he was dominated by Jesus. Spurgeon was the greatest preacher of modern times, but he was dominated by Jesus. John Knox made the queen fear his prayers more than the armies of Scotland, but he was dominated by Jesus. John Calvin told the libertine he would preach Christ even if they slew him in the pulpit, but he was dominated by Jesus. Martin Luther said as he went to the Diet of Worms, "If every tile on every roof turns to devils and comes against me, I will still stand for Christ." But Luther and the best men of all ages were dominated by Jesus.

Listen to these words: "Here was a man born in an obscure village, the child of a peasant woman. He grew up in another obscure village, where he worked for 30 years in a carpenter's shop. For three years he was an itinerant preacher. He never wrote a book. He never went to college. He never owned a home. He never traveled more than two hundred miles from where he was born. He never set his foot in a big city. He never did things which accompany greatness. He had no credentials but Himself.

"While still a young man the tide of public opinion turned against Him. His friends ran away from Him. One denied Him and another one turned Him over to His enemies. He went through the mockery of a trial. He was crucified between two thieves. His executioners gambled for the only property He had, a coat. When He died He was taken down and buried in a borrowed tomb through the pity of a friend.

"Nineteen centuries have come and gone. Today He is the centerpiece of the human race, the leader in the column of progress. All the armies that ever marched, all the navies that were ever built, all the parliaments that ever sat, all the kings that ever reigned, all put together,

Jesus, Highest Over All

have not affected the life of man on this earth as powerfully as that *one solitary life of Jesus.*"

I dropped into a barber shop in another city one day to get a haircut. When the barber learned that I was a minister, he began a bitter tirade against the church, ministers and church members. When he had finished that tirade I asked him the question, "But what do you think of Jesus Christ?" And he answered, "Oh, He is second to none." We may have our faults and our methods or messages may often fail. But there is nothing wrong with Jesus. He is highest over all. Follow Him and you'll never go wrong.

Some years ago I had occasion to visit a doctor in Chicago. I saw a number of religious books in his reception room. When I went in to see him, I asked, "What church are you a member of?" He answered, "I was reared a Catholic. I now belong to a Presbyterian Church. But I am, reading the philosophy of Buddha and I like him best."

Then I said, "Oh, doctor, Jesus is high above Buddha and all the great men of the world. Follow Him and all will be well with you now and forevermore." And I say to you as I said to the Chicago doctor, "Follow Jesus and all will be well."

12

What Jesus Means to Me

I Peter 2:7

Simon Peter was a man who had been "through the mill." He had his thrills and his spills, his joys and his jolts. He was often on the mountaintop and often in the valley. He had his trials and his triumphs. He was a saint and a sinner. But as he looks back on it all, we hear him saying, "Jesus is precious to me." Like Peter, we, too, have had our ups and downs, our good days and bad. But all of us can say, "Jesus is precious to me."

There are two kinds of knowledge. There is the knowledge that we gain by what we hear or what we read. Then there is the knowledge that we gain from actual experience. The latter knowledge is the best. So Peter speaks out of experience when he says, "Jesus is precious to me." And all who have had that experience with Him can also testify that He is precious.

David said, "Let the redeemed of the LORD say so" (Psalm 107:2). The angel who met the woman at Jesus' open tomb said to them, "Go and tell." The apostles went to their death telling the story of Jesus. Paul stood before kings and slaves and told of his conversion. Jesus meant something to him and he did not hesitate to tell it. If He means anything to us, we, too, should be always telling the old, old story of Jesus and His love.

I. Who Is This Jesus?

1. *He is the prophesied One.*

The prophecies concerning Jesus began in Genesis, where God said that Jesus would bruise Satan's head and Satan would bruise the heel of Jesus. In Isaiah 53 we are given the greatest picture of Jesus to be found in the Old Testament. "He was wounded for our transgressions, he was bruised for our iniquities; the chastisement of our peace was upon him; and with his stripes we are healed" (verse 5).

In Isaiah 28:16 He is spoken of as the foundation stone. In Isaiah 32:2 He is spoken of as a "hiding place." In Isaiah 9:6 He is called the "prince of peace." In Job 19:25 He is spoken of as our "redeemer."

He is called the "rose of sharon," the "one altogether lovely," the "chiefest among ten thousand," the "King of kings and Lord of lords." All the prophets sang of Him. And when He came He fulfilled in His life and death and Resurrection all the prophecies concerning Himself.

2. *He is the sacrificed One.*

The highest One in heaven laid down His life for the lowest ones on earth. He was "the lamb slain from the foundation of the world" (Revelation 13:8). It is true that He died on Calvary, but in God's mind and in His own He was sacrificed from the foundation of the world. He loved with a sacrificial love, He lived a sacrificial life, He died a sacrificial death. It was all for us. Our sin was great, therefore the sacrificial offering for our sin must be great. Jesus became that sacrificial offering. Now we realize that "where sin abounded, grace did much more abound" (Romans 5:20).

Do you remember the story of Abraham and Isaac? God told Abraham to go up to the top of the mountain and offer up his son on the altar. God was simply testing Abraham's love for Him. Well, Abraham obediently made the altar ready and placed his son on it, although his heart was breaking. He loved that boy, but He loved God more. As he lifted the dagger to plunge it into the heart of Isaac, God called out, told Abraham He was satisfied and furnished a ram for the sacrificial offering.

We had sinned and the knife of eternal condemnation was raised to slay us. But Jesus came forth as a Substitute and that alone saved us. "God commendeth his love toward us, in that, while we were yet sinners, Christ died for our sins" (Romans 5:8).

3. *He is the saving One.*

He said, "Look unto me, and be ye saved, all ye ends of the earth" (Isaiah 45:22). We read that "there is none other name under heaven given among men, whereby we must be saved" (Acts 4:12).

What does a drowning man need most of all? He needs a rescuer, a Saviour. When we were going down to hell Jesus came forth, saying, "I will be your Saviour. I will reach down and pick up that sinner and set his feet upon the rock of ages." Yes, He does save unto the uttermost all who come unto Him by faith.

A dear old Scotchman lay dying. He was a great Christian. No one could get any response from him as he lay in a coma. His pastor leaned over to him and whispered, "Sandy, dinna ye ken your wifey?" But he made no answer. Then the pastor said, "Here's your daughter. Dinna ye ken your wee daughter?" Still there was no response. Then the preacher leaned a little nearer and asked, "Sandy, dinna ye ken Jesus?" And the old man opened his eyes and his face lighted up, while he said, "Aye, I ken Jesus. He is my ain dear Saviour." Yes, Jesus is the saving One. In life and in death we are saved by Him.

4. *He is the helpful One.*

He does not save us, then leave us in the eternal struggle of life. He says, "Lo, I will be with you unto the end of the way." He is with us in our sorrows and our joys. He is with us in our temptations, ready to strengthen us if we turn to Him. He is with us in our homes, in our work, everywhere.

Psalm 46 tells us that He is "a very present help in trouble." Just look back over your life. There has never been a time when He was not right there, ready to help.

> I know not where His islands lift
> Their fronded palms in air,
> I only know I cannot drift
> Beyond His love and care.

II. WHY DOES JESUS MEAN SO MUCH TO ME?

1. *Because of what He has done for me in the past.*

(1) *He died in my stead.* I had broken the law, I deserved nothing but death, that cross was meant for me. But He went to the cross in my stead and suffered all the pangs of hell for me.

A ship was floundering in the middle of the ocean, her engine broken. The passengers were in peril of death. When the captain asked for a volunteer to go down into the steam-filled engine room and make the necessary repairs, a young man offered his services. Soon the trouble was all over and the passengers were safe. "Lets go down," said the captain, "and see about our friend." When they found him he had breathed his last breath. The passengers paid for his burial and on his tomb they wrote, "This friend died that we might live." My soul was going down, I was eternally lost. But Jesus came from the shining shore and died for me. Oh, that's the greatest love ever shown in this world.

(2) *He led me to see my sin.* The devil blinds us to the fact of sin. The average unsaved man doesn't realize that he is a lost sinner. But the Bible says that he is "dead in trespasses and sin" (Ephesians 2:1). Jesus led me to see that about myself. He showed me that I was a sinner and that my sin was taking me to hell.

(3) *He washed that sin away.* How could He pay the price for my sin hundreds of years before I was born? Well, suppose you bought your groceries on credit at a certain store. Then one day a man walked into that store and placed a million dollars to your credit. This would cover all your debts and all that you could ever owe. Christ went to the cross and shed blood that was so precious He could say, "This blood will pay for all of your sin, past, present and future."

I have walked by the seashore when the tide was out and have left my footprints in the sand. Later the tide came in and washed those footprints entirely away. So does Jesus cover all my sin when I trust Him as my Saviour.

2. *Because of what He is doing now.*

(1) *He helps me to overcome temptation.* Not one of us is perfect and at some time we will be tempted by Satan in the fiercest manner. But we have an outside power to help us to overcome. He "will not suffer you to be tempted above that ye are able; but will with the temptation also make a way to escape" (I Corinthians 10:13). But often when temptation comes we don't cry out for help and it is then that we falter and fall.

> Take the name of Jesus ever,
> As a shield from every snare;
> If temptations round you gather,
> Breathe that holy name in prayer.

(2) *He answers my prayers.* There have been many things I have been called upon to do, things far beyond my capability, but He has helped me in a thousand ways.

When God called me to preach I had gone through only two years of high school, and had gone to work to support myself and family. I met discouragement on every side, from many people. But the Lord was with me. He answered my prayers. I was able to finish high school on the outside and was then asked to preach my own commencement sermon. With a wife and two children I was able to go through college and seminary, my prayers being answered in a marvelous way. Without Him I could do nothing. I could never stand up and preach in my own strength, but with His help I have ministered for more than forty years in His Name.

Jeremiah 33:3 says, "Call unto me and I will answer thee, and shew thee great and mighty things, which thou knowest not." John 14:14 says, "If ye shall ask any thing in my name, I will do it." He simply gives us a blank check and tells us to draw on the bank of heaven. He gives us a master key and invites us to open the door to His storehouse of blessings. He is great in answering prayer.

(3) *He is comforting and leading me.* Oh, He knows how to comfort. He was "a man of sorrows and acquainted with grief." And because He walked through the vale of tears He knows how to comfort those who sorrow.

One of our young couples lost their tiny babe and I conducted the quiet little funeral service. The next Sunday the young father said to me, "Pastor, I am closer to God than ever before." Another one of my members lost her teenage daughter. Her heart was broken but she said, "Pastor, what would I do now if I didn't have Jesus?" And I wonder what we would do in the dark hours if we didn't have a Saviour to whom we could turn.

Jesus knows how to comfort as no one else. He knows

how to lead us, sometimes beside the still waters, sometimes through the dark valleys. He has promised never to leave us or forsake us.

I pity the man who must travel the rough roads of this life alone. Some years ago Dr. L. R. Scarborough conducted a revival in the church where I was pastor. One day we went together to a man's office to talk to him about his relationship to Christ. He showed very little interest. We were not able to win him to the Saviour. Several weeks later this man went into a restroom in the bank and blew his brains out. He didn't have a Comforter and Guide to bless and direct his life.

One of my friends tells about a tragic thing that happened at Niagara Falls. He said that he stood there with his wife and others, gazing upon the beauty and majesty of the falls. Suddenly a couple who stood there put their arms around each other and leaped to their death at the foot of the falls. But one who has Christ in his heart need not despair like that. Even when the going gets rough he is not alone.

(4) *He is giving me hope.* The lost man has no hope. His is an awful state. He looks out into the future and all he can see is an impenetrable darkness.

Dr. J. Wilbur Chapman one day visited a prison in Ohio and talked to the inmates there. One man had been there 37 years. Dr. Chapman asked him if he would like to be free. The man replied, "Why should I wish to be free? My friends are gone, my family is scattered. I have nothing to live for." He was an example of a man without hope. But Jesus gives a man hope. He bids us to trust Him for today and then tomorrow will be better.

3. *Because of what He is going to do.*

(1) *He will be with me in the hour of death.* "Yea, though I walk through the valley of the shadow of death,

I will fear no evil; for thou art with me" (Psalm 23:4). Oh, if you are a Christian you need never fear death. Death will be only a change for the better, a translation from the land of tears into the land where God shall wipe all tears away. Paul said, "For me to die is gain" (Philippians 1:21). Yes, we gain infinitely more in death than we can ever gain in life. We gain freedom, we gain fellowship, we gain fulness of knowledge, we gain everything good when death takes us out to be with the Lord.

We sing, "Asleep in Jesus, blessed sleep, from which none ever wakes to weep." We sing about being "safe in the arms of Jesus." We can't sing these songs if we don't know Jesus.

(2) *There will be no condemnation for me.* Romans 8:1 says, "There is therefore now no condemnation to them which are in Christ Jesus." When a criminal faces the court, he fears the consequences. But if a friend pays his fine out of court, he has no fear. Oh, we should be condemned. We have sinned, we have broken God's laws, we have trampled the Son of God under foot. We deserve nothing but condemnation and hell. But, praise God, we have a Saviour who will save us from all condemnation.

(3) *There will be no hell for me.* I deserved it. "The wages of sin is death" (Romans 6:23). But when I took Christ as my Saviour, He put the lid on hell and nailed it down forever as far as I am concerned.

(4) *Then one day I will be like Him.* I may go up out of the world to meet Him in death. Or I may go up to meet Him in the air when He comes back. No matter how I go, when I meet Him, I will be changed in the twinkling of an eye. I shall be like Him. What a miracle that will be! What a glorious prospect!

(5) *Then heaven is waiting for me.* I get tired here, I have trouble here, I suffer pain and heartache here. But

none of these things can touch me when I get to heaven. In His presence there are joys evermore.

Now you may ask, "Will Jesus be a Friend to me?" Oh, yes, a thousand times, yes. He longs to be your Saviour and your Friend. Millions on earth and millions in heaven above can testify that Jesus is the best of all friends. Let me introduce you to Him. Repent of your sin and put your trust in Him and He'll be your Saviour and Friend forever.

During the Civil War a wounded boy lay in his tent. His mother traveled a great distance to see him, but the hospital authorities would not permit her or anyone else to go into his tent. So the mother slipped around to the back of the tent. She could hear the groans of her son and it broke her heart. She reached her hand under the side of the tent and placed it on the boy's head. The groanings ceased. The boy said, "That feels like my mother's hand." And peace and quietness flooded his soul.

Is your life tossed about in sin and strife? Well, Jesus is just waiting to lay His hand on you and give you peace. He waits now to forgive your sins and plant your feet on the road that leads to heaven and home.

Will you go on without Christ and go to hell? Or will you let Him be your best friend? The choice is yours. Your happiness and your destiny depend upon it.